INSTRUCTOR'S GUIDE TO

The *Lexington*
Introduction to Literature

Lois Josephs Fowler
Kathleen McCormick
Gary Waller
all of Carnegie Mellon University

D. C. HEATH AND COMPANY

Lexington, Massachusetts   Toronto

PREFACE

The editors of The Lexington Introduction to Literature bring together a variety of critical approaches—but probably no less broad and contradictory than the instructors who will use it! We are united by the desire to make the recent advances in literary theory adaptable to the classroom through the curricula and pedagogy by which literature is taught. We disagree, usually harmoniously, on some of the methods to use and the extent to which theory has a place in the classroom. Paradoxically, perhaps, we hope that this harmonious disagreement is reflected in this Instructor's Guide, because the equivalent variety of views is presumably reflected in its users. For those instructors well versed in post-structuralism, some of the material here may seem old-fashioned; to those who are not, it may seem unnecessarily theoretical. That contradiction not only reflects the varied instructors who will use the Lexington Introduction: it also reflects the contradictions within the whole profession at the present time.

In practical terms, these contradictions will, we expect, prove useful: many of the questions or discussions of the texts are written from different critical perspectives. While we hope that all the assignments and teaching notes reflect the theory set out in the Lexington Introduction, their perspectives vary. There is a blend of formalism, "subjective" reader-response criticism, historical and biographical approaches, as well as the distinctively reader- and culture-centered perspective central to the Lexington Introduction. Although it is the last category that we hope will become the dominant one whenever this text is taught, the former will give all instructors ways into it. We believe this eclecticism will help make the text accessible to a wide variety of instructors.

We direct your attention, as well, to the book Reading Texts, also published by D.C. Heath (1987), written by two of the editors, Kathleen McCormick and Gary Waller, with contributions from their colleague Linda Flower. Instructors and students of any literature course will find there an extension and application of the theory that informs the Lexington Introduction to Literature.

We wish to thank our indefatigable research assistants, Laurie Walz, Jennifer Even, Jackie Hall, and Karen Gray, for helping us put this Guide together.

Contents

Reading and Responding to Drama

Reading and Responding To Essays

Anthology of Essays

A Sample Syllabus with Teaching Notes and Writing Assignments

INTRODUCTION

Lexington Introduction to Literature, for which this Instructor's Guide is designed, is the first of its kind. As readers of its introduction will quickly discover, we believe that literary (and other) texts get meaning not through their inherent qualities alone but interactively through the matching of the repertoires (literary and general) of both text and reader. This is a theory of understanding literature that has been gaining acceptance rapidly in the field in the past decade or so. In addition to their arguments about its value as a theory, the authors offer here a device for teaching it effectively in the classroom. This device is the **response statement**, to be used by the student in progressively refined and elaborated stages, including the longer paper.

While the application of the theory in the Lexington Introduction may be to some extent novel, the authors believe that it is easy to understand and rewarding to use. It is often difficult for college students to bring their own experiences to bear on the interpretation of literature and, even more important, to discover in the process why they respond as they do. In the Lexington Introduction and this Guide, theory and practice place heavy emphasis on the readers' own contribution to literary meanings, encouraging them to enter into a dialogue with the text in systematic ways. The result is to make classrooms livelier and students' writing richer.

The Lexington Introduction's choice and arrangement of texts have been kept generally conventional. Selections are drawn largely from the established canon, organized by the usual genres of fiction, poetry, drama, and essay, and ordered chronologically within these categories. These arrangements make it convenient for teachers to locate selections when organizing their own syllabi. An instructor who prefers a syllabus with a chronological arrangement, for example, might begin with Antigone, move to some medieval poems, then turn to Hamlet and Elizabethan poetry, and so on, linking the different genres as they paralleled one another in given eras. Or an instructor who wished to organize a course topically, perhaps choosing feminism as one topic, might again begin with Antigone, follow it with Renaissance carpe diem poems, and go on to nineteenth-century poems such as Browning's "My Last Duchess" and stories such as Maupassant's "Miss Harriet" or Kate Chopin's "Regret," and then to a variety of material written by and about women in the last thirty years. Gender-specific questions for such an approach abound in the Reading and Responding section. Materials for such a topic need not necessarily encompass the whole chronology or, for that matter, be arranged chronologically at all.

In the final section of this Guide readers will find a detailed syllabus for a one-semester course based on the material in the Lexington Introduction. This has developed from the experiences of the authors and their doctoral students in teaching these materials in an introductory literature course, "Reading Texts," at Carnegie Mellon University.

Teaching the Five Introductory Essays

The Lexington Introduction's introductory essays--the general introduction, "Becoming a Strong Reader," and those essays that open the sections of the book on the several genres--provide strong but carefully explained theoretical statements about the meaning and interpretation of literary texts. We recommend that they should be read, analyzed, and discussed by students like any other critical essay. The teacher might, in fact, add to the syllabus other critical essays that have proved provocative, especially ones which add viewpoints reinforcing those here. Critical essays can be used at any point in the course, depending on the character of the class and the preference of the instructor.

Although each of the Lexington Introduction's essays makes use of many examples, the instructor may wish to add other pertinent ones in guiding students through them. Here we provide some general strategies for teaching these essays and specific questions for teaching each essay.

GENERAL STRATEGIES

1. Assign short, relevant parts of an essay for reading and subsequent class discussion as you teach the literary texts.

2. Read and explain some especially important or difficult sections of the essays aloud in class.

3. Use essays in conjunction with the literary works suggested in them and add others as they seem suitable for the needs of your particular class.

4. We suggest the following order of activities in teaching the essays: first, questions pertaining to direct comprehension of the ideas of the essay; second, questions about literary selections that illustrate the ideas of the essay; finally, questions that allow students to challenge or amplify the ideas in the essays.

5. Very early in the course, carefully go over the general introduction on writing Response Statements so that students can see how to write them.

QUESTIONS FOR THE GENERAL INTRODUCTION: BECOMING A STRONG READER

1. What is the approach to reading outlined in "Becoming a Strong Reader"? What is the relationship between text and reader? The relationship among reader, text, and theory? Explore the relationships among reader, text, in the new paradigm in literary study.

2. How is the term "ideology" used as it applies to the interaction of reader and text? Discuss the meanings of "reading situation," "dominant ideology," and "literary ideology."

3. What meanings do the terms "general repertoire," "literary repertoire," and "matching of repertoires" have as they apply to the reading of a poem? Have students discuss in class the diagram and apply what they learned in reading to a short story, perhaps to "The Yellow Wall-paper."

4. How does the meaning of a text change over time? How is that change defined in the relationship between reader and text? You might wish your students to read Raymond Williams's essay from Keywords at this point to illustrate this aspect of theory.

5. How are the terms "gaps" and "indeterminacies" applied to the strategies readers use when they read?

6. What does it mean to do a strong reading? (Here we suggest that you illustrate this notion by reading and discussing Blake's "The Tyger" and Kundera's "Hitchhiking Game" because both easily evoke a diversity of strong readings.)

7. What elements should exist in a good response statement? How do you react to the sample extracts from the student response statements on "Crazy Jane Talks with the Bishop" in the introductory essay, and how would you write a response statement to this poem?

8. Why is it important to reread? Reread "Counting the Mad" to see if this strategy changes your initial response to the poem.

QUESTIONS FOR THE FICTION INTRODUCTION

1. What does a reader bring to a work of fiction? What factors influence the way a reader responds to historical and cultural contexts in reading fiction? (Perhaps use Faulkner's "A Rose for Emily" for its cultural context and "Young Goodman Brown" for its historical context as illustrations.)

2. What is meant by "literary repertoire"? Discuss that term in relation to such conventions of fiction as plot, character, point of view, and theme.

3. What is meant by the expected and unexpected unfolding of events? How is the "unfolding" of a narrative related to its sense of reality? How do you naturalize a text which does not unfold in chronological

order? (Use "The Cask of Amontillado" and Stein's "As a Wife Has a Cow" to discuss these questions further.)

4. What strategies do you habitually use in order "to make meaning" of a text? In what way do you use the point of view of the narrator to help build consistency?

5. Discuss some of the ways a student can move from a response statement to writing a formal paper.

6. In what ways do the expectations about genre that readers bring to a text influence the way in which they read that text? (Use Calvino's "The Canary Prince" and Kafka's "Metamorphosis" to illustrate how students have strategies for reading the former but may not necessarily have strategies for reading the latter.)

7. What sorts of social/cultural issues may be raised in a work of fiction? Discuss racial issues as they are raised in Morrison's "SeeMotherMotherIsVeryNice." (Here instructors may also want to read and discuss the racial issues in Ellison's "Battle Royal" and Petry's "The Winding Sheet" to illustrate further the way different general repertoires interact with fiction on the questions of race and ethnicity.)

QUESTIONS FOR THE POETRY INTRODUCTION

1. Discuss your students' notions about the purposes and ways of enjoying poetry. Are there limits to what poetry can be about? Read and discuss Daniels's "Short-Order Cook" to focus discussion on some of the issues that can be treated in a poem.

2. What does this essay say about author's intention and its relationship to meaning? How do you respond to the position taken in the Poetry Introduction on the question of authorial intent?

3. What strategies do you habitually use to build a response to a poem?

4. How do you build a strong reading of a poem? What specific strategies do you use? Discuss the strong reading of Blake's "The Tyger" in the introduction. Do you agree or disagree with it?

5. Explore some of the uses of metaphor, especially in poetry. Discuss allegory (relate back to "Young Goodman Brown"), simile, symbol (use Hopkins's "Spring and Fall"). Discuss a surface reading of this poem, then a variety of strong readings.

6. How do readers' different repertoires produce different readings of a

poem? What is meant by a harmonious matching of repertoires? Do you necessarily like a poem better if your repertoire closely matches its?

7. How does a reader produce a strong feminist reading of a poem? Do you create with that kind of reading of Wyatt's "They Flee from Me?" (We suggest that where it seems appropriate, students read some of the contemporary feminist poetry of Rich, Plath, and Piercy at this point.)

QUESTIONS FOR THE DRAMA INTRODUCTION

1. What is the difference between the play as a text and the play as performance? In what ways do you develop multiple meanings of a play as text? Or of a play as performance?

2. Why is drama considered the most "open" of all literary forms?

3. What makes drama distinct from fiction? What characterizes a play? A script? What kind of information does the reader get compared to that in fiction?

4. What is the difference between a fixed text and a working script? How is that difference manifest in readings of Hamlet?

5. Discuss the multiplicity of critical readings of Hamlet. Find critical interpretations of Hamlet to supplement the ones in this essay. Share these in class and then discuss how this added information influences your initial perceptions of Hamlet.

6. What does it mean to have an ideological engagement with a play? (Here we suggest that students may read Rosencrantz and Guildenstern Are Dead or Death of a Salesman to illustrate further what ideological engagement with a text can mean.)

QUESTIONS FOR THE ESSAY INTRODUCTION

1. How can you define an essay as literature? What are the various ways in which one can define literature?

2. Is there a distinctive language for literature? Can literature be written in what you think of as "ordinary" language?

3. What are some of the reasons for reading essays? What is the difference between discursive prose and referential prose?

4. How can a reader distinguish reading "through" a text from reading "at" a text?

5. Read the section on "Illness as Metaphor" in the Essay Introduction, looking at the questions, then at the whole essay. Explain what metaphor is, how illnesses are used as metaphors, and respond to some of the issues Sontag raises.

6. How are ideology and language related? How does this relationship influence what the authors of the Lexington Introduction call "the political unconscious"? (Here we suggest that students read Williams's and Harris's essays to see, in more depth, how language changes among cultures and over time.)

7. Compare Williams's definition of "individual" with Crevecoeur's.

Reading and Responding to Fiction

In this section, we provide notes for instructors who have asked students to respond to the assignments in the "Reading and Responding to Fiction" section.

LYNNE BARRETT, "INVENTORY": ADDITIONAL RESPONSE ASSIGNMENTS

This is a good story to direct students to examine their own reading strategies, especially those they take for granted as "natural." A story like this looks as if it should be taken "literally," as a slice of life. Students can all "relate to it," "identify" with the characters, recognize the "same" kinds of experiences.

In fact, most readers already possess conventionally learned reading strategies for such a story. The response statement questions direct students to some of these, and the title provides another prompt. To help students read the story's setting metaphorically rather than literally, ask them to explore the expectations they bring from their general repertoires on warehouses, department store sales, counting items of merchandise, and then to try to transfer these metaphorically to Patty's new life, as a worker, as a woman, perhaps (some students might speculate) as a student. Key points for many readers will be the meeting with Mr. Wold, the reminiscences about Cherrybeth, and of course the exchanges with Eddy.

The question about the ending can be used to direct students not only to the what-happens-next aspect, but also to Barrett's strategy of leaving the story open-ended. What does that do for a reader? What assumptions do readers have if they expect a story to tie all the ends up? In short, without discouraging your students from "interpreting," encourage them to see how their reading strategies have been developed out of previous literary experiences with this kind of story (a comparison with Raymond Carver's "Cathedral" is apt here) and from their general repertoires.

FRANCES PERKINS GILMAN, "THE YELLOW WALL-PAPER"

Direct your students to the different effects that different narrative voices tend to produce. Use of the first person tends to ask for closeness or "identification," encouraging personal association rather than summarizing (compare "Lives of Girls and Women"). The third person omniscient often makes a reader seem more passive, but third person limited or an unreliable third- person narrative should make readers more active and suspicious. Get your students to trace their different routes through the story, showing how they become aware of any unreliability in narration. If they have difficulty recalling other fiction that uses such a technique, direct them perhaps to Emily Bronte's Wuthering Heights, Henry James's The Turn of the Screw, John Barth's "Lost in the Funhouse" or Oates's "Lady With the Pet Dog." Perhaps raise the question of whether any narrator "really" knows what's going on--any more than any author does.

D.H. LAWRENCE, "THE ROCKING HORSE WINNER"

Focus on how the story seems to require a set of strategies a little like those used with a fairy story, except that the setting is "realistic." This can open up a discussion of the techniques of "magic realism," some of which operate in the story. The easiest way to understand the term "magic realism" is as a kind of joke on realism in which absurd events or characters are introduced for comic effect. The result is a hybrid that combines magic, myth, or the absurd with narrative. Consider the appeal of this combination to children (as in such books as Sendak's Where the Wild Things Are).

Although the effect of "The Rocking Horse Winner" is not comic, it does combine elements of the realistic and the fantastic that may require students to develop new reading strategies. (You might compare "The Rocking Horse Winner" with Barthelme's "Porcupines at the University," which uses the techniques of magic realism in different ways.) A few students will always take a rigidly "literalist" position and find the story puzzling or stupid, as with Kafka's "The Metamorphosis." Such students have a distinctive set of reading strategies in their literary repertoire that don't satisfactorily fit this story: it can be read literally only by ignoring its "magical" aspects, such as the mouse's talking or the boy's insights. A literal reading may try to explain these away as hallucination or coincidence.

Whether your students read literally or allegorically, try to get them to be conscious about the strategies they are adopting and why. Don't forget to point out that their "moral" interpretations inevitably develop from either privileging the "realistic" parts of the story and/or allegorizing the fantastic.

MILAN KUNDERA, "THE HITCHHIKING GAME"

This story has proved especially good at provoking discussion on such issues as power struggles between men and women, how relationships can suffer from too much fantasy, or the pains of growing up. In bringing their own experiences to the story, students typically come up with a variety of responses: the woman had to find a way to break out of her primness; both were victims of media stereotypes; everyone plays roles of one kind or another but they went too far; games can become dangerous when the difference between reality and illusion becomes unclear.

Students familiar with Freudian theory might relate the events of the story to dreams and their sexual content. You could explain manifest and latent dream content, and open a discussion about the genetic/social/metaphysical reasons underlying deviant sexual drives.

Obviously the story can lead to a discussion of how students feel about the relationships between men and women, sexual power struggles, and the need for and enjoyment of power. Are women trained to yield to power? Would active feminism mean that those differences would disappear along with the pressures for women to fit such stereotypes?

7

RONALD SUKENICK, "THE BIRDS"

The discussion of this story generally concentrates on the form of the story, especially on what aspects of life that form tends to imitate. Some students find that the fragmentation of the story makes it nearly impossible to read, while others like it and talk about the way in which it imitates the unpredictability of life.

Some students will find the story frustrating and stupid. Probe the students who dislike it to explain why. Is it their limited experiences with unconventional fictional forms? Can they expand their repertoires by adding new strategies for reading? Some may say that the story is held together like music, with the recurring references to birds, foods, and freedom acting as motifs.

You could raise the question of whether all the details of a story must fit. Ask students how many kinds of literary elements they can identify in the fragments, whether handbooks on birds, trashy romances, "shaggy dog" stories, or newspaper cuttings. Then compare it to a collage. You might discuss whether in fact this story is much closer to the texture of experiences of the eye than "realistic" stories. And don't forget to ask about the ways in which they find the story funny!

Anthology of Fiction

We follow here the order of the stories found in the <u>Lexington</u> <u>Introduction</u> except for those used in the "Reading and Responding" section, which have already been discussed. Since you will probably not be teaching all the stories, we have usually made the discussions self-sufficient.

NATHANIEL HAWTHORNE, "YOUNG GOODMAN BROWN"

Response Statement Assignments

1. To what extent does your religious repertoire, especially your own concepts of sin and guilt, affect your reading of "Young Goodman Brown"? How do your beliefs make you either want Goodman Brown to proceed on his intended journey or to retreat from it?

2. Hawthorne set "Young Goodman Brown" in the colonial period but wrote it in the mid-nineteenth century. Does your "reading" of the colonial period differ from his?

3. Do you read Goodman Brown's journey literally or metaphorically?

4. How would you react to this story if the names of the main characters were changed: say, Peter for Goodman Brown, Joan for Faith, and Susan for the Widow Cloyse?

Teaching Notes

General Repertoire: Many of our students like the story, and are entertained by it on one level, but when asked to consider the intellectual and specifically the religious issues, find its delineation of the evil nature of mankind offensive. "We are not all that evil deep inside," commented one student. This was said in response to another who felt that we ought not to look so deeply—<u>not</u> go into the forest—because of what we might find. You may find this a good story to illustrate how students' repertoires of religious beliefs help form their reading.

History: You can ask why Hawthorne used Puritans in New England in order to tell his story, since it's not like a conventional historical story, or even, seemingly, interested in the historical setting. Tell students something of Hawthorne's background in New England, of his own Puritan ancestry, and of his interest in the witch trials of Salem and their implications for good and evil in human nature. His own time, the middle of the nineteenth century, shared those interests but approached them in a more secular fashion, viewing virtue more as its own reward than as a way of getting to heaven. Hawthorne layered the perspectives of both centuries, and modern readers necessarily add their own perspectives. You might point out how the seventeenth century is like any other "text," always to be read in the light of the questions that different ages, and different readers, draw from their own repertoires.

Metaphor: Have students reread the passage in the poetry section on metaphor, which explains how readers interact with the text's use of figurative language. Certain obvious parts of the story--the ribbon, the forest, the names, the walking stick--can easily be read allegorically (allegorical reading is also covered in that discussion of metaphor). Pose the question of whether a reader must read the story on this level, since you will generally find a group of "literalists" in a class who will resist doing so. What do students feel are the advantages of the different types of readings they can give the story: a literal reading--it really happened; a figurative reading--it's an allegory pointing to the good and evil in all mankind; a naturalization of the story in which the supernatural is explained away as natural--it was only a dream? You might also ask how the characters' names lend themselves to the use of metaphor and allegory. Focus on such questions as: What do you think might happen to you if you somehow journeyed into your deepest, unconscious mind to discover what was there? Into the minds of those around you? How do you think Hawthorne's nineteenth-century America regarded such a symbolic journey? How do you regard it? How much do you want to know about your innermost thoughts?

HENRY JAMES, "THE REAL THING"

Response Statement Assignments

1. How did you respond to the artist's dilemma when he realized that Miss Churm, his model, looked more like "the real thing" than did Major Monarch and his wife?

2. How did your repertoire of social expectations prepare you to react to the setting and relationships of the story?

3. How does this story meet your expectations about the conventions of narrative? Focus especially on your response to the relationship between what you are told about the couple and what you are shown.

Teaching Notes

Nostalgia (Clash of Repertoires): "The Real Thing" reflects a sort of Old World culture in which elegant gentlemen and ladies inhabit a world of leisure and "blankness," such as "the twenty years of country-house visiting that had given them pleasant intonations." But the Major and his wife have lived as visitors on the estates of others, having no money of their own. James wrote about these people as living at the turn of the twentieth century. Ask students whether they could find anyone like them today.

Stereotypes (Literary Repertoire, Textual Strategies): We tend to center our discussion of this story on the conflicts between reality and illusion. Television stereotypes provide good illustrations here. Students may point to the way the media produce stereotypes and expectations of the rich and famous, to the degree that seeing them portrayed in magazines or on television is in itself counterfeit. This can lead to a discussion of how the narrative conventions of the story affect readers' responses. Some students might consider that these conventions made the artist uncomfortable because he, too, had a set of stereotypes about how he himself would act with such people and how they ought to be depicted to the public. The whole concept of the "real thing" may seem problematic given the way the characters are depicted. Students may also speculate about what might happen to people like the Major and Mrs. Monarch, whose main strength seemed to consist of having upper-class style. You can focus on the deeper ideological assumptions behind image and illusion.

GUY DE MAUPASSANT, "MISS HARRIET"

Response Statement Assignments

1. Guy de Maupassant writes a story within a story, a literary device with which you are probably familiar. How does that device affect your reading?

2. Critics have seen "Miss Harriet" as a story which illustrates the power of men and its misuse, and the resulting weakness and suffering of women. Construct a strong feminist reading of the story.

3. Compare your responses to the issues raised in this story with those you find evoked by Margaret Atwood's "Loulou; or, The Domestic Life of the Language." What differing textual strategies do you find in the two stories and how do they affect your responses? Which do you find more relevant today and why?

4. Whose responsibility is Miss Harriet's death? In formulating your answer, comment on how your own repertoire helps produce it.

Teaching Notes

Feminist Readings: Both this story and Atwood's "Loulou" provide excellent opportunities for raising the question of how to construct a strong feminist reading. Often men will feel that Chenal did not have any responsibility for Miss Harriet's death, while women in the class may respond very differently and see him as sexist in his attitudes toward women, in the pride of masculinity that emerges in his gestures, and in the way he tells his story. Some students will argue that society is responsible for Miss Harriet's death, as she has been socialized to be a romantic and to devalue her looks; similarly, some may argue that in flirting with her and boosting his own male ego, Chenal too is a product of a sexist ideology.

Narrative Style (Text Strategies): The following questions are relevant here: What do you bring from your own past experiences with stories--either telling them or hearing them--that influences your response to their narrative strategies? In what way do the storyteller and his audience heighten the drama of the story? How do the listeners, for example, become a part of the whole story they are hearing as well as a part of their own setting? Does a device such as this one reflect a reality that links you with the events around you? How? Some students may find the storytelling device confusing and unnecessary. Some, however, may note that it is an effective way of providing multiple impressions of Chenal, through both his interaction with the group he was with and his remembrance of the story in his past. You can use such observations as a basis for a general discussion of narrative style. How does one decide what to believe in a narrative? What does one bring to the text from previous literary experiences? How does the text influence what one brings to it?

KATE CHOPIN, "REGRET"

Response Statement Assignments

1. The meaning of the title of this story, "Regret," is a major gap that you have to fill in. At what point in your reading did it become clear that you had to fill it?

2. Does Chopin provide all the information needed to make Mamzelle Aurelie's final loneliness seem logical, or does she count on what the reader brings from his/her own experience? What did you bring from your repertoire as the narrative unfolds?

3. What difference does it make that the protagonist is a woman and not a man?

4. To what extent do you find yourself constructing a "plot" for the story? How much is given by the text?

Teaching Notes

The Title: In discussing the meaning of the title as an important gap that readers gradually become aware they must fill, you should let the discussion first dwell partly on such text-based questions as whether or not Aurelie made a mistake. What constituted the core of her life? What was entertainment or fun for her? Then broaden the discussion to include students' repertoires. What aspects of her life seem like fun to them? Would a woman like Mamzelle Aurelie, who seems to have enough money, have more options if she chose to remain unmarried today? She could have a child even if she were to be a single parent. How do you feel about that option today for someone who suddenly discovers that she misses having children in the house and has the money to care for them but is unmarried?

Genre and Structure: It might be argued that the story is a "woman's story," one of mood rather than events, perhaps like stories told by students' grandmothers or mothers, told them when they were children. Would one hear the same kinds of stories today? That question may evoke responses about how times have changed, how people, even women, are busier than ever. You might also focus on the implications of the last description of Mamzelle Aurelie: "Oh, but she cried! Not softly, as women often do. She cried like a man, with sobs that seemed to tear her very soul." Why such loud sobs? Why are such sobs like those of a man and not of a woman? Are softer, smaller sobs more appropriate for a woman? Does Mamzelle Aurelie seem masculine in other ways? What determines students' ideas about what is masculine/feminine, especially in their reactions to grief? How often do they see men cry on television? As often as they see women cry?

Ideology: Other discussion might focus on the cultural implications of how people rear children. You could compare what Mamzelle Aurelie learns about children to what her neighbor instructs her to do when she leaves them. Assumptions about how children behave normally, including how they respond to different kinds of treatment, is central to such a discussion. Some of our students see the Mamzelle's methods as too simplistic, arguing that they won't work because children need more discipline along with love, while others disagree. Discussion can focus on students' individual attitudes as they emerge from a variety of broader culturally derived assumptions and experiences.

Expanding Students' Repertoires: You might supply students with information about the late nineteenth-century culture within and about which Kate Chopin wrote, and about the recent discovery of Kate Chopin as a writer because of the new interest in forgotten women writers who have been neglected. You might provide some introduction to her novel, The Awakening, about a woman married to a rich Creole man and her search to find a meaning in her life. This kind of discussion sometimes moves into feminist interpretations of fiction, of gender-specific responses to stories like "Regret," "Inventory," and "Miss Harriet," to see how male and female responses to these stories might differ or how the current feminist movement might have affected them. Adrienne Harris's essay on language and baseball will also be helpful here.

STEPHEN CRANE, "THE BRIDE COMES TO YELLOW SKY"

Response Statement Assignments

1. How does your knowledge of the literary or textual conventions of the Western story affect your reading of this story?

2. What ideological assumptions found in the Western affect your reading of the story?

3. How do your tastes in humor influence your reading of the story?

Teaching Notes:

Genre and Ideology: Students are generally interested in talking about the conventions of the Western story and about the relationships between their concepts of that genre and the Crane story. Many of them realized that Crane, like other writers of Westerns, could count on certain expectations from readers about that form. Introduce the ideological dimension of the Western: students generally know that ideology quite well. Students may comment that bringing a new bride to the frontier is central to the plot of many movies of this kind. Do your students expect that intimate details of the characters' relationship should be presented? Do they feel these details are not necessary because they don't expect much communication between men and women even when they love each other? Or is that merely a convention of the Western? Some students may dislike the story for just that reason—too many gaps, not enough explicit information. This kind of discussion may move further into the conventions of the Western. Readers may tend to expect stereotyped personalities and characters in a Western while expecting more detailed character development in a seemingly more realistic story like "Miss Harriet."

You might also discuss the conventions Crane did not use in "The Bride Comes to Yellow Sky," and ask whether the story could be seen as satirizing the Western. One reader will see it as satire, another as gently humorous. If this story were turned into a movie, what sort of music would convey the intended atmosphere? Where would the movie probably be filmed?

The American historian Frederick Jackson Turner wrote that the frontier in American history was the most important factor in providing independence for Americans, a place for men to go where they could make a living on their own, without a boss. Women also used the frontier as a way of finding more independence than they could have in the East, where options for marriage and jobs were few. Ask what special codes were expected of people who decided to make this kind of life their own. What kind of a life was it? How do the students respond to "American Individualism" as the characters in this story illustrate it?

Structure: Westerns tend to encourage their readers to adopt conventional reading strategies. You might ask students whether they like detective stories, mysteries of one sort or another, or science fiction. These genres, in some ways removed from daily life, supposedly allow us to relax, to enter a world of unreality, away from everyday concerns. The narrative form of this story compares well with that of "Miss Harriet." While the story is told in conventional style, it moves back and forth in time, beginning in the present, then returning to past events in order to explain the present, then to characters' thoughts, which set up the possible conflicts of the immediate future. In this way Crane moves the plot toward the final confrontation.

Humor: An easy way to get into discussion is to ask: does the story make you laugh, smile, think? Readers differ on just what is funny in "The Bride Comes to Yellow Sky": attitudes toward women? strained relationships between men and women? codes of honor among men? definition of courage? Probing more deeply, you can get students to discuss their own response to that humor in terms of their own comic stereotypes. If they don't think the story is humorous, do they see it as dated?

JAMES JOYCE, "THE DEAD"

Response Statement Assignments

1. Who or what are the "dead" of the title?

2. Did you read the story literally or metaphorically? What do you feel you must have in your repertoire, both general and literary, to read this or any other story symbolically?

14

3. What aspects of your cultural repertoire, such as your knowledge of Ireland at the time Joyce was writing, your knowledge of Joyce himself, your knowledge of Catholicism, your experiences at Christmas dinners or with love relationships, influence your reactions to the story?

Teaching Notes

Literary Repertoire: This is sometimes a difficult story for students to read, as many think it goes nowhere. It can, however, provide an excellent opportunity for students to articulate and expand that aspect of their literary repertoire that makes literal and figurative distinctions. This subject is frequently dealt with in discussions of poetry, but its significance as a reading strategy with fiction is often ignored and can be demonstrated with this story. The tone of the story is realistic and hence possibly seems literal, yet all of the events, descriptions, and most of the characters' names can be read symbolically. This story is most frequently read as highly symbolic, focusing on the contrasting images of light and fire, and cold and snow. The title "The Dead" can refer metaphorically to living persons, such as Gabriel, Kate, Julia, and Gretta, as well as to those who are literally dead, like Michael Furey, or Ireland in general. Let the students discuss the particular aspects of the story they read symbolically as much as possible. They might focus on a single scene, like Gabriel's speech, or his confrontation with Gretta, or on a particular character, or on the references to Ireland throughout the story, or on the various contrasting images of fire and cold. Discussion could include examining the various colloquial phrases appearing in the story such as: "She /Gretta/ must be perished alive;" "Mrs. Malins will get her death of cold"--cliches that can be read as richly connotative. Students might focus on the symbolism of the snow: cold yet blanket-like; exciting because it's Christmas, yet also death-like, particularly at the end of the story, when it is "general" all over Ireland.

Multiple, Contradictory Meanings: It is important that students recognize that moving from literal to figurative reading opens a text up to many contradictory meanings. Therefore the goal of the class ought not to be developing a consensus about what the story really means, but understanding that it can have simultaneously contradictory meanings, depending on the assumptions and strategies the reader is bringing to bear. Symbols are created by ways of reading; they are not inherent in the text. Emphasize that nothing is intrinsically symbolic just as nothing is intrinsically ironic. Encourage students to articulate and analyze the assumptions, literary and general, that make them choose (consciously or not) to read the text in a particular way.

General Repertoire: The previous question provides a transition into discussing students' general repertoires. Encourage students to discuss in detail any information or experiences they feel influence their responses to the story. Let the students open up the discussion--even do some free-associating about the story if necessary--so you can help to lead them to recognize: a) that there are differences in their general repertoires; b) that these differences may in part account for some of the differences in their responses to the story.

FRANZ KAFKA, "METAMORPHOSIS"

See Discussion in The Lexington Introduction, pp. 52-53.

WILLIAM FAULKNER, "A ROSE FOR EMILY"

Response Statement Assignments

1. How does your general repertoire affect your reading of racial relationships in the story?

2. At what points did you start to realize that something was not quite right? At what point in your reading did you realize what was "really" going on?

3. Outline the process by which you built up a portrait of Miss Emily. What did the text contribute? What did you contribute from your own general repertoire?

4. If you were asked to write a version of this story for television, what parts of it would you stress for visual effects? Would you show some of the scenes that you, as reader, only hear about?

Teaching Notes

Consistency Building: We begin our discussion of this story by telling students about the geographical area, the American South, that Faulkner usually wrote about and of some of the characters who reappear in his work. We sometimes introduce sections of The Sound and the Fury or Absalom, Absalom to the class so that they can reflect on the versatility of Faulkner's style. This is a good way for them to see that writers who can compose a straight narrative often choose not to do so. So we discuss narrative style and why Faulkner may have chosen the style he did for "A Rose for Emily". Like Poe's "The Cask of Amontillado," this story pulls the reader along slowly but relentlessly towards the final horror. These tales reflect what in literature can be called the "gothic" tradition of mystery, crime, revenge, and the supernatural. Ask your students to respond to that tradition as they see it used in "A Rose for Emily." Ask which narrative structure they prefer and why.

A Feminist or a Cultural Reading: Much has been written by critics about Miss Emily as a character. In developing a strong reading of the story, you might suggest to students that they analyze Emily from either a feminist or a cultural perspective, or from a combination of the two. How does Emily's being female and living in the South during a particular historical period constrain her behavior? What motivates her? Anger at Homer Barron? Expectations of what men should be like, of how loyal they should be? Her relationship with her father? Her high-powered pride? Her inability to change? Is she perhaps just a bitter woman who, having been rejected, has gone insane? Can and do people like Emily exist today? Some students may comment that Miss Emily couldn't help being the way she was because of her socialization. Others may find it is difficult to reconcile her pride with her liking for Homer

Barron, who was socially beneath her. Still others might argue that Emily's killing Barron was like killing all of the new social forces that she refused to adjust to.

History: Many of Faulkner's stories and novels take place in post–Civil War Jefferson, Louisiana, where the war changed the economic but not the social status of many of the very rich. Perhaps students have learned in other classes, or from their own experiences and other reading, about the culture that produced the peculiar strength of belief and action that Miss Emily possessed. Do the students respond to the changes of attitudes in the next generation, with its more modern acceptance of social flexibility? What about the role of her servant, "the negro," and that of Colonel Sartoris who "remitted" Miss Emily's taxes but "who fathered the edict that no Negro woman should appear on the streets without an apron..."?

ERNEST HEMINGWAY, "HILLS LIKE WHITE ELEPHANTS"

Response Statement Assignments

1. Ernest Hemingway is noted for his elliptical, terse narrative style. How do you respond as a reader to a writing style that forces you to fill in so many "gaps"?

2. Trace how the significance of the title developed as you read.

3. Show how your views on abortion affect your reading. Did reading the story in any way either weaken or strengthen your initial attitude?

Teaching Notes

Ideology--The Abortion Issue: Students almost always want to begin with a discussion of the abortion issue, which many of them see as central to the theme of this story. Why this should be so is worth discussing as an example of ideological conflict in our society. Those students who are very much against abortion see "Hills Like White Elephants" as reinforcing their attitudes and produce strong readings accordingly. Not only do they not see any reason for this couple to have an abortion, but they feel strongly that both the man and woman were, and would continue to be, depressed by the abortion. Students who define themselves as pro-choice, however, will frequently feel that the story was not really about abortion, but rather about the lack of communication between the lovers. Such an issue, therefore, is ideal for showing the interactive nature of making meanings as well as for demonstrating that themes are "created" by readers, not "found" in texts. Almost all students agree that both lovers have an inability to communicate, but whether they see the story as being about this inability to communicate seems to depend on their view of abortion.

Narrative Strategies: Ask your students if they like a story that recounts very few events and gives sparse dialogue, with very little information regarding what characters may be thinking. There has been much critical disagreement about the dramatic force of so "terse" a style. We found that our female students were more dissatisfied with the style than our male students. "This is more like

17

a sketch than a story," commented one woman, "I have no sense of these people's motivations." But many of the men disagreed. "Why do you need that much information? We get what we need to know about the situation and the plot is simple but well defined." Many of the men—not all—liked Hemingway's style, his speed in getting to the point, while many of the women did not because they wanted more detail. The strategies behind such readings seem often to be curiously gender-based. Some of us have used the section of Carol Gilligan's In a Different Voice, in which she talks about the differences between male and female responses to moral dilemmas. She concludes that men tend to respond according to a set of moral codes, while women tend to respond in "a networking style," in which they consider all of the factors within a context, including everyone involved in it in order to make a judgment.

Title: We suggest you ask students to focus on the relationship between the title and the words of the woman at the end of the story. "I feel fine," she said. "There's nothing wrong with me. I feel fine." Ask your students what the title means to them and how they feel about their responses. A standard response is that readers' vagueness of feeling while reading the story and getting to know the characters—despite disagreements about taste—parallels the vague outlines of hills in the distance that could resemble large animals.

ANN PETRY, "LIKE A WINDING SHEET"

Response Statement Assignments

1. Show how your reading of "Like a Winding Sheet" relates to your own repertoire of ideas and feelings about the nature and cause of violent feelings.

2. Show how your views of racial issues contribute to your reading.

3. What in your own repertoire can you relate to the lifestyle and the work situation depicted in the story? Do your own expectations about the quality of your life conflict with the reality of the situation presented in the story?

Teaching Notes

Matching of General Repertoires: Many questions relating to work expectations and roles open up here. Some will be racial or gender-specific, others class-based, and you will inevitably find different matchings of repertoires occurring. Some readers will see this story as dated because people rarely work ten-hour shifts today and because Johnson could not be refused a cup of coffee in most places. But presumably work situations like Johnson's, even if the working hours have decreased, could be equally frustrating today. Seeing the relevance of some part of the text's general repertoire to their own, such issues arise as: Is frustration and boredom an inevitable part of life? Is Mae simply more tolerant of frustration than her husband is? Are Johnson's expectations related to his being male?

Our students often opened class discussion by talking about the relationship between Mae and her husband. The title, "Like a Winding Sheet" appears when Mae laughingly tells her husband, as she wakes him up, "You look like a huckleberry—in a winding sheet." What does she mean and how does he respond to it? Is his losing control and beating her the only way he can exert the power he needs to feel? Does this suggest anything to students about the problem of battered wives? Men in the class may feel that Mae, despite the fact that life was hard for her, had no real understanding of her husband's problems, and that she almost pretended not to see how uncomfortable and miserable he was. Such readings do not see this situation as a feminist issue, but rather as one having to do with how people respond to others' needs. The ideological assumptions underlying such a response need to be probed.

Some students may argue that the geographic area in which they grew up influenced their differing attitudes on racial issues, but frequently disagreements about other aspects of the story—filling in gaps about Johnson's background, understanding how this husband and wife had differents sets of expectations, and perceiving the difficulty males had in dealing with female authority—were based on gender rather than regional differences. There will probably be agreement that although "Like a Winding Sheet" was written before some of the social changes we now have, problems such as the frustration and degradation of the poor, the exploitation of blacks by whites, power struggles between men and women continue to exist.

Reading Strategies—Character Preference: That it is Johnson's story rather than Mae's will probably be generally agreed upon in your classes, though a number of students may want to follow up what happened to Mae. Does she go to a clinic for battered women? Can a person love after an experience like this one? Is it possible to live with Johnson and really believe he has changed or will one always live in fear? It is his story, they agree, but they feel uneasy about the end, not knowing whether Mae lives or dies. This is not just an ideological issue, but one of reading strategies. The narrative, though straight and simple, may be, to some students, unsatisfying because of its perspective. Such an approach to the story can help to develop a strong reading of its point of view by raising such issues as: Why it is told from Johnson's perspective? Whether Mae's silence in the story is indicative of her powerlessness in the relationship and further of the general powerlessness of many poor women? Whether the story's being told from Johnson's perspective suggests that he possesses greater power or authority than Mae or whether it ironically indicates his inability to articulate his anger and to act out his aggressions in a positive manner?

RALPH ELLISON, "BATTLE ROYAL"

Response Statement Assignments

1. What, in your own attitudes about racial or feminist issues, makes you respond as you do?

2. At what points in the story did you find yourself preferring a "metaphorical" to a "literal" meaning?

3. Consider the ideological contradictions in which the narrator is caught.

Teaching Notes

Ideology--Racial Issues: Ralph Ellison's "Battle Royal" is one chapter in his long novel, The Invisible Man, which draws on his own transition from innocence as a boy in rural Oklahoma to experience of the realization of what it means to be black in a white culture. In our classes, discussion almost always begins with the focus on both racial and feminist attitudes as students respond to how "Battle Royal" makes them feel: angry, frightened, sorry, even guilty, but never complacent. In 1965, when segregation and situations like those Ellison depicts in "Battle Royal" did exist, thousands of people from all parts of the United States joined in movements to attempt to change those conditions. Ask students whether a story such as this one would have prompted them to act?

Title and Metaphor: Ellison fuses realistic details with a host of metaphors. How do readers respond to that mix? Does it heighten the dramatic force of the narrative or make it artificial? What is the impact of such metaphors as "battle royal" or "invisible man," or "Live with your head in the lion's mouth"? Do they blend well with "the school superintendent" who yells, "Bring up the shines" or with the description of the woman? Yet within those realistic details, some students may argue that "shines" also functions as a metaphor, as does the description of the woman with "hair...yellow like that of a circus kewpie doll" or "breasts...firm and round as the domes of East Indian temples..." Just what does this particular mix in the use of language imply?

The meaning of the title Invisible Man is a question that often arises in class. How can one perceive oneself as invisible? What are the implications of that concept in both literal and metaphorical terms? Students show a great deal of interest, especially when we mention the H.G. Wells novel of the same name and its implications for the nineteenth century. Here we find that Ellison's story provides a good way of talking about the interaction of metaphors and social issues. The discussion went on from there to how Ellison's rhetoric and that of others--whether of the political right or left--influenced readers and listeners.

JOHN BARTH, "LOST IN THE FUNHOUSE"

Response Statement Assignments

1. What reading strategies did you adopt to cope with the narrative style in the Barth story where the sequence of events is not ordered, where the narrator intrudes to discuss with the reader what he might have his characters do next?

2. As you reread the first lines of the story, do they conform to your expectations about the life of an adolescent? Do they remind you of yourself at one point in your life? How do your gender and family experiences influence the nature of your response?

3. At what points did you feel that you had to choose to read the "funhouse" literally? At what points did you read it metaphorically? What did your decision contribute to your reading?

Teaching Notes

Reading Strategies: Students usually (and often with puzzlement) fall into a discussion of the narrative style of the Barth story because most have fairly conventional expectations of narrative. They expect narrative flow to be interrupted by dialogue, or perhaps by a description of a character and what that character thinks, or of a place and time. They even feel comfortable with a narrative in which a character remembers something of the past or when the narrator fills in details of the past. But they are generally made uncomfortable by a narrator who talks about how to write a story--largely because such a convention is new to them and they do not have any strategies for reading it.

You should therefore encourage a detailed concern with writing and reading strategies--if only because Barth builds in so many textbook instructions! Ask such questions as: How does such a style challenge your expectations of how a story is told? Do you feel you are being manipulated when the author intrudes to ask you, the reader, how he should end the story? How do you respond to the questions that the narrator poses to the reader? Do they interfere with your concentration on the events in the story? (A comparison with Pirandello's Six Characters, if you are studying drama, might be useful here.) What feelings does this narrative style evoke about the "theme" of the story? Barth's style might be read as an attempt to illustrate the way life really is (a widespread assumption about fiction which students should probe), not organized according to a conventional linear plot. Some students find that the instructions about writing a story provide a humorous touch to the seriousness of growing up, while others think it irrelevant and contrived. Behind the two views are very different assumptions about reading fiction. What seems to generate agreement is that Barth's approach is designed to make fiction more rather than less realistic in its suggestion of what it means to live in this culture. Whether that method succeeds or not seems to depend very much on the repertoire of reading strategies students bring to it. Here it is most important that they see not just how they respond but why. Students who have read more "postmodern" fiction (or have studied the fiction chapter in Reading Texts) have something in their repertoires that helps them with this story.

Metaphor: What the funhouse means also generates discussion because funhouses are fascinating places. "There is no texture of rendered sensory detail, for one thing," says the narrator. How does the reader respond to that statement within the context of the funhouse as Ambrose wanders? dreams? thinks? distorts? confesses? Ask your students why they think people like to go through a funhouse, a place of distortion, and what experiences of this kind of place they bring to the story? Some students may remember being afraid of getting lost in funhouses in amusement parks. Like Ambrose, they may recall feeling that their lives had enough inconsistency in them already, and see the funhouse as an effective metaphor for the confusion of adolescence. In addition to being a metaphor for adolescence, the funhouse can also be a metaphor for the experience of reading the story, with its distortions and multiple angles of vision. You might try to get students to link the various connotations of funhouse. In what ways is reading the story like experiencing adolescence? In what ways is reading the story fun? In what ways is it disturbing? What kinds of people like to "get lost in the funhouse"? What kinds of people unwittingly find themselves "lost"? Explore with your class the multiple connotations of these questions.

ALICE MUNRO, "LIVES OF GIRLS AND WOMEN"

Response Statement Assignments

1. How do you respond to the way in which the thoughts of the narrator and the events of the story build to expand your first impression of the title?

2. In what way does your gender influence your response to this first-person narrator?

3. How do you respond to the quality of life in such a town? How does the description of this town differ from or confirm your own expectations of small-town life?

Teaching Notes

Gender: Sexuality is usually the main topic of discussion with this story. Obviously the initial focus is on the narrator. What has she learned about her own sexuality, and sexuality in general? Ask students what they perceive as the difference between her final reaction and her mother's advice? Have them look at that advice again. Do they agree or disagree with it? Would their response be like the narrator's? Above all, pose the question: how does their gender influence their response? In what way do they see a generation gap between mother and daughter? Are such differences apparent to them in their own family relationships?

Alice Munro is known for her perceptive depictions of a variety of women. Ask the students which of the women in this story they find most interesting. Which one would they most like to know? to meet? to see? In what way are Fern, Naomi, or the mother different from the narrator? What do they have in common? Why does Fern change? How has her life been damaged--because she had the wrong/right ideas about what fun really is? What makes Naomi's interest in sexuality change? What does her relationship with the doctor have to do with that change? Does that kind of situation strike you as realistic? Has she matured or just become frightened or disillusioned?

In addition, responses to Mr. Chamberlain are certainly worth investigating because he seems, in one way or another, to be at the center of all these women's activities and thoughts. Ask the students how they fill in the gaps of his relationship with Fern? Do they see him as worth her caring about? Why does she seem to care about him, and even want at one point to marry him? Why doesn't he sexually exploit the narrator, or is his masturbation in front of her a kind of exploitation? Is his sending her to find the letters he wants a kind of exploitation? Is he the kind of man you like? feel sorry for? look down on? hate?

Power and Maturation: There are other issues that will probably engage students. These are problems of power, and of defeat, cynicism, and disappointment, especially in the lives of women.

Ask what students think of the poems that the narrator finds in Fern's room when she is looking for the letters. You might get a variety of responses to this question: she was sexually frustrated; she engaged in fantasies because of having no real sex life of her own; she was the product of small-town morality, of living with hated boundaries that she was afraid to break. Many of our students who knew something of Freud saw her as symbolizing repressed sexuality. One woman, however, insisted that while Munro's repertoire clearly had Freud in it, she was able to go beyond Freud in having the narrator make a decision about her life, and so grow, but without really understanding what lay beneath that decision.

Jubilee is a small town in which everyone seems to gossip, to know one another, to be concerned with what their neighbors do. The narrator's mother gets excited when she finds out that Mr. Chamberlain has been to Florence, even if only during the war. She knows "the Medici and Leonardo. The Cenci, The cypresses..." and she shows him the statue of David to find out if he has seen the original. Her excitement fails when, in response to her comment about decadence, he can only remember that a man offered to sell his daughter to him for a fee. Clearly she means something quite different. Why then do you think she stayed in Jubilee? Why did Fern Dogherty stay there? Why did Chamberlain leave? How do you respond to the quality of life in such a town? How does the description of this town differ from or seem like your own expectations of small-town life?

Reading and Narrative Strategies: Focus on such questions as whether the story develops in a consistent pattern. Ask your students how they would define that consistency? Do they find it predictable or surprising? Do they find themselves engaging in consistency building at key points? You may get general agreement about the success of the first-person narrative used in this story. Some students will like this story better than "Lost in the Funhouse," which also uses the first person, because their repertoires allow them to deal better with the straightforward movement of the narrative and the narrator's telling the story directly to the reader. Others may prefer the Barth because of the humor and find Munro too serious and even exaggerated.

DONALD BARTHELME, "PORCUPINES AT THE UNIVERSITY"

Response Statement Assignments

1. Do you find "Porcupines at the University" funny or do you read it more seriously?

2. What strategies do you adopt in dealing with the characters and the situation?

Teaching Notes

Literary Repertoire: Students probably know the TV comedy program Monty Python's Flying Circus. Allow them to discuss the parallels in textual strategies

23

between the two.   You can also tell them something about theater of the absurd, about how it attempts, through absurdity, to offer new perspectives on the real.   In attempting to define reality, the theater of the absurd employs absurd situations to dramatize that meaning of reality.   Ask your students if they think Barthelme does that.   If your students tend to take this story seriously you can also talk about existentialism.   Here the fact that one has little control over much that happens in life influences strongly the definition of reality.   To existentialist thinkers, the real is the other; one knows one's own existence only through others.

A Possible Strong "Serious" Reading: During the 1960s, there was a great deal of protest at colleges in the United States over social issues, focused increasingly on the war in Vietnam. Donald Barthelme lived through those times of deep controversy.   While Barthelme presents his story in a light and funny manner, inviting readers to laugh at the absurd juxtapositions, a few students, accustomed to looking for serious "themes" in fiction, might be initially puzzled by it unless some kind of "serious" reading like this is provided.

Humor: But to most students, a solemnly "strong" reading such as that suggested above may seem perverse.   A better approach may be to focus on the Monty Pythonesque absurdity.   They can fantasize about seeing a horde of porcupines coming across their college campus, even sitting in their college classroom.   How would they respond to a sight like that?   How do they think the Dean or the President might respond?   What in their expectations of college, of the instructors and administrators, does Barthelme count on so the reader will react and fill in the gaps that make the story funny, interesting, unusual?   Why do they suppose the story begins with the Dean's saying, "And now the purple dust of twilight time/steals across the meadows of my heart..."?   Does anyone remember the Platters' 1958 hit, "Twilight Time"?   Does that reference date the Dean?   One of the editors of this guide?   When the scout, whoever that is, yells that the porcupines are coming, the Dean then says in a rather calm fashion, "Maybe they won't enroll," while he decides what to do and while his wife points out that they are not people.   How do they respond to what seems like an absurd situation and absurd people: a Dean who decides to shoot the porcupines and a wrangler who has fantasies about making money?   All these questions should evoke a common part of their repertoires--television black humor.   Some of your students, indeed, may have even read some of Barthelme's stories in the New Yorker and elsewhere and be familiar with his kind of humor.

JOYCE CAROL OATES, "HOW I CONTEMPLATED THE WORLD FROM THE DETROIT HOUSE OF CORRECTION AND BEGAN MY LIFE OVER AGAIN"

Response Statement Assignments

1. In what way does the title set up your expectations for how the story will be told?

2. How do you fill in the gaps in the story? Focus on the characters: did anything in your literary or general repertoires make them seem familiar?

3. How do you react to the variety of socio-economic groups in "How I Contemplated..."? to the variety of socio-economic settings? With whom, if anyone, did you identify yourself?

4. At the end, is the narrator really home?

5. How do you respond to the narrative style of the story, the "notes for an essay for an English class"? Did you think when reading the story that the events were really happening to the narrator or did you think she was just making them up for her English assignment? Were you able to create a plot, a consistent movement toward the narrator's coming home?

Teaching Notes

Psychological Repertoire: Many of our students have written about the significance of the narrator's final comment that she will never leave home again. They argued over what "home" really meant. To some students it may mean love, which they did not see in her home, but rather her life with Simon or in even in the house of correction where coldness would be expected. "Her parents seemed interested in her as if she were an object," commented one of our students, "so no wonder she left what was supposed to be a home." But other students will disagree with that viewpoint, and argue that she was clearly spoiled by her perhaps too materialistic parents. Perhaps she seems directionless to some, or a person who is pulled in the most immediate direction. Many students who respond this way to the narrator may notice that the narrative style seems to parallel the rather hazy personality of the narrator.

Social Repertoire: Focus on the issue of class, the significance of which the narrator is largely unaware except in material terms. There is some hint, for example, that Simon, like 'he narrator, comes from an upper middle-class family, but generally the reader fills in the many gaps about why the characters behave as they do. Do they respond with sympathy to Clarita or to the narrator's father? Which groups do they think the narrator refers to, "poking around in debris; disgust and curiosity..." in the subtitle? How do the various kinds of doctors fit into those socio-economic groups? What is the response to the time spent by the author on these various doctors? What is your response to the time and attention they give to Princess? Many students may feel that the narrator, living in her fine house on the rich street, was in a childish way trying to understand those who have less then she does.

Narrative and Reading Strategies: Oates's story is an excellent introduction to disruptive narrative, unreliable narrators, and the way readers must bring their literary as well as general repertoires into play. You should encourage discussion of the expectations, not only of the title, but also of the titles of sections such as "Characters We Are Forever Entwined With." Is this serious or ironic? Ask students how the title sets up their expectations for what is to follow: satire, humor, serious discussion of the meaning of life. Is this story supposed to be "really" happening? Does it matter to students whether or not the narrator has "made everything up"? Are students' expectations about the nature of fiction challenged, disappointed, exactly in line with their discoveries as they read the story? Still others read many of the sections as suggestive of the trauma of growing up, especially with insensitive parents who give their children only money. Why do "World Events" get such dismissal? Can the narrator be trusted--even at the end?

RAYMOND CARVER, "CATHEDRAL"

Response Statement Assignments

1. What is the effect on your reading strategies of the first-person narration? How involved do you find yourself? Do you believe the narrator?

2. What strategies do you adopt with the style of the story?

3. At what key points did you find yourself wanting to read metaphorically? What difference did that make to your reading?

Teaching Notes

Style and Narration: Part of the problem with a seemingly transparently "realistic" story like this is that readers are tempted to fall back on naive reading strategies and talk about the characters as if they were real, about relationships and "themes." As with Lynne Barrett's "Inventory," it is therefore especially good for examining those apparently "natural" strategies for reading, and getting your students to become more self-conscious about them in their repertoires. Do they like the narrator? Do they feel that they are expected to like him? What is their sense of why he seems so ambivalent about the blind man, about his visit? Do your students think he really has the stereotypes he professes to have about the blind? "In the movies, the blind moved slowly and never laughed." Does his telling of the story provide readers with insights about the kind of person he is? Does he seem to think in stereotypes about other things? You can push such questions in the direction of personal association. Do your students feel uncomfortable when they are with someone who is blind? Thus you can ask your students: How do you respond to the way in which the author behind the narrator seems to treat blindness? Does that treatment bother you or do you feel it to be sympathetic? Why is blindness treated in such an unexpected way in this story? Does that treatment defy your expectations in some way?

Metaphor: But, more interestingly, many readers will increasingly adopt metaphorical readings, believing that a story this simple must have a "deeper" meaning! Why is this moving from the "literal" to "metaphorical" level such a typical reading strategy? How many of your students made that move? Why? Do their expectations about "literature" influence their reading strategies? In other words, direct them back to their own expectations. They may respond well to a discussion of literal and metaphorical blindness. Some students may see this story as one about communication problems and may agree that drawing the cathedral was the narrator's path into seeing what he had not seen before.

Some readers tend to read this story as humorous, as satirizing how people act in social situations--a kind of absurd reading of what life tends to be about. Again, there will be a temptation to thematize this interest. What is absurd? Perhaps the blind man is more comfortable, more at ease, than the man who is not blind.

MARGARET ATWOOD, "LOULOU; OR, THE DOMESTIC LIFE OF THE LANGUAGE"

Response Statement Assignments

1. How did you react to the title? Why? How did the story meet or not meet your expectations? What kind of a woman does the name "Loulou" make you think of? What in your general repertoire makes you think as you do about that name and the subtitle? Do your responses to it change as you read the story?

2. What is the significance of the narrator's comments? Does your gender affect your response after Loulou has sex with the accountant?

3. How do you respond to the differences in social class between the poets and the accountant in "Loulou"? What would you do if you were Loulou? How do you think your own social class position influences that response to this question?

4. You have learned something about literary theory as you have worked with the Lexington Introduction. Probably you understand what the poets are talking about when they give Loulou all sorts of names. What do you think they mean when they discuss the language which is "different from just words: it has this mystical aura around it, like religion, she can tell by the way their voices drop reverently whenever they mention it." It continues with one of them saying, "I'm really getting into the language." Why do they do that? How do you respond to her response to them?

5. How do you like the tone in which this story is told? Are there indications to you, other than the name on the story, that the narrator is a woman? What do you think about the notion of gender-specific language? While the narrative is third person, it is told from Loulou's point of view. How does that point of view contribute to your response to the story, its irony and humor?

Teaching Notes

Title and Social Class: Many of our students were interested in discussing the title of the story because they wanted to sort out the connections they found between Loulou and whatever "the domestic life of the language" meant. Some felt that it could be taken in a literal sense, that is, the story of a woman who shares her domestic life with a group of poets who become her children--she nurtures them in every way possible. One student suggested that although the story raises issues about male/female relationships, so too does it address the class difference between the person of craft and the person of words.

Gender: This story is especially good for getting students to examine their own gender-based reading strategies. You might focus on the implications of Loulou's change from a quiet discontentment that sends her out looking for different kinds of men to a kind of satisfaction with her living situation. Some of our students found her to be very innocent and therefore able to be exploited by the poets even while being revered by them. Yet other students see her as somewhat more in control of her own situation: "Loulou is someone who commands respect, who is strong, who satisfies her own sexual needs, and who comes out a heroine," said one student. Another saw her as fairly strong and independent, with or without the poets. "They really cared for her; the accountant treated her like an object," said one young woman, "so she goes back to where she's comfortable and loved even if somewhat exploited." "But she's too innocent to go further," answered another student. "She would be exploited wherever she goes." If you get responses such as these, try to get the students to focus on their own gender-specific reasons for having them.

Style (Literary Repertoire): Most students like having the story told from Loulou's point of view because they feel that getting her thoughts, even if indirectly through the third person, allows for the humorous contrasts between her innocent but practical nature and the poets' innocent and impractical natures. Students tend to be comfortable with what they term the "reality" of the style, something you might have them examine more closely.

ANN BEATTIE, "SHIFTING"

Response Statement Assignments

1. Ann Beattie's style resembles speech rather than what is generally perceived to be "literary" language. How do you respond to the straightforward and almost casual narrative style?

2. What political issues underlie the tensions in the story? How do you respond to the differences among the ways these people see relationships?

3. How does your response to Natalie's having sex with Michael reflect your gender and attitudes toward sexual morality?

4. Consider the ending of "Shifting." What will happen next, do you suppose? What makes it dramatic—or don't you think it is dramatic? Do you care what happens to Natalie, Larry, or Andy? What aspects of your literary repertoire help you to imagine the continuation of the story?

Teaching Notes

Narrative and Style: Some students may want to talk about the narrative style: some will like it because it is immediate while others will find it dull. Focus, perhaps, on the title—do your students read it literally? What does "literal" mean here? Some will see that shifting the gears of a car is like the shifting in Natalie's life. Some students find this to have an inherent drama—her movement, after marriage and adolescence instead of before, into her own sexuality. So you might find there is discussion and disagreement about where she might be headed next.

Political Issues: Some of the questions you might use to focus your students' attention include: Why does Natalie not want to see Andy? Do you suppose her feelings have something to do with her warning him not to go to Vietnam? Or is she just too wrapped up in her own thoughts and needs? What is the difference between the way in which she sees the world and the way in which Larry, his parents, and Andy see the world? In what way do you think that Michael's perceptions differ from those of the other characters? Is he just younger or does he have a different sense of how things should be when he says, "I thought it was funny that he didn't teach you himself, when Mrs. Larsen told me you were married."

Students understood the clash of ideologies over lifestyle and the Vietnam War; they even realized that Natalie would, in her way, probably go far beyond Larry and Andy in their still conventional approaches to life. But there was general agreement that Andy handled his disability in a brave way and that she should have respected him for that. A few students felt that she had a right not to see Andy if she felt that his physical state could have been avoided, had he been more critical of a romantic notion of duty to his country in that kind of a war, but most disagreed. They seemed to feel that his patriotism made sense to him and that his physical condition called for support. While they worried about Larry's carting him off to a bar, they applauded Larry's concern that Andy was lonely. "Maybe Larry even feels a bit guilty because it didn't happen to him," said one of our male students, as he went on to explain that although his older brother had been a conscientious objector and did not participate in the Vietnam War, he felt somewhat guilty when he saw a veteran who had been seriously injured.

Ideology: Beneath the political issues are deeper ideological ones and you can usually draw them out. That Larry and Natalie had not discussed who they would vote for in the election seems a serious problem in their marriage. Does that relate to the students' sense of the importance of politics? Ask students about the relationship between ideological clashes and communication in marriage, and its connection with sex. Is "Shifting," then, a story about the shifting ideology of one partner in a marriage in which the other partner does not move?

ALICE WALKER, "NINETEEN FIFTY-FIVE"

Response Statement Assignments

1. How do you like the first-person narrator of this story? What is there in your own repertoire that brings about your response?

2. As you read, what are your expectations of what the story will be about when Traynor and Deacon first come to Gracie Mae Still's door? Does anything in your own repertoire make you think that they are about to cheat her? As it works out, can you develop multiple interpretations of who is really cheated?

3. Alice Walker is known for her ability to recreate the reality of Southern black culture. What is your response to the racial implications of this and other scenes in the story? Of the stories in your literary repertoire, both from this anthology and other reading, which one makes you the most angry about racial intolerance?

4. How do you respond to the humor of the story? Discuss how your own sense of humor matches or clashes with that of the story and how that affects your reading of it.

5. Traynor never does understand what the song means. Why not, do you think? What do you think it means even from what you hear about it? Why does Traynor continue to try to understand? Why do his fans act in the way they do to make him uncomfortable? Do their responses have something to do with their attempts to understand the song--with what attracts them by the song even though they don't fully understand what that attraction is? Why does Traynor continue to send gifts to Bessie? Is there some connection between his sending of these gifts, his confused notions of materialism and happiness, and the meaning of the song? How do you respond to the implications of his confusion?

Teaching Notes

Intertextuality: We tell our students something about Alice Walker and many of them will have seen the disappointing but popular movie of her novel The Color Purple. Thus the story provides a good example of intertextuality. Since that version is available on videotape, you might perhaps play it for them so that they can follow Walker's development from "Nineteen Fifty-Five" to the film. You might have them read the novel too if possible, because students can explore how an author develops her writing style and they can also compare visual and verbal media. Most of our students loved "Nineteen Fifty-Five" and saw the narrator as a combination of Celie and Shug in The Color Purple. What they concentrated on here also was the way Walker brings this culture alive by her delineation of the way characters live, think, and feel. The letters in the story, for example, reminded some students of the epistolary style of the novel. Students felt that Walker's imitation of the spoken language kept the reader absorbed in the relationship between what was said and the way it was said.

Identification: A fairly common response to characters is for students to say they "identified" with them. The assumptions behind this are worth probing. You might focus on the text's strategy, asking: How do you see Bessie? What does she look like, especially as she grows older? Do you think that you, unlike the audience on the Carson show, would enjoy the way she sings? How much do you know about jazz, or about Bessie Smith, the famous singer of blues? How do you respond to the way she perceives her world, even what she says she doesn't understand? How would you define her repertoire? Would it be, in any way, a materialistic one? And why, even though she is quite fat, does she never have any problem getting a man to love her? Above all, get your students to focus on what in their own (mainly general) repertoires created their reactions.

Ethnic Issues: Both the humor and the ideological conflicts (especially focused on Traynor) can become interesting points for discussion. Do your students see any parallels between Traynor and famous rock stars like Elvis Presley or Marvin Gaye, who died tragically? How do they deal with the distinctively ethnic-based humor of the story?

Reading and Responding to Poetry

In this section, we provide notes for instructors who have asked students to respond to assignments in the "Reading and Responding to Poetry" section of the Lexington Introduction.

PHILIP LARKIN, "CHURCH GOING"

Whether or not students go to church or temple, or whether they think of themselves as casual or committed religious believers, their lives and inheritances have been deeply influenced by both the power of institutional religion and the secularization of the modern world. So initial reactions to the poem will probably be provoked by the title.

In the case of most American students, however, the church (the building as opposed to the institution) does not often convey the sense of a long tradition or a venerable civilization. The reading strategies such students might use to deal with Larkin's poem might include expanding their repertoires very consciously by historical research, or perhaps by creating a strong reading from the perspective of an inhabitant--whether religious or secular--of the New World. Such a reading should also produce a greater tolerance for ambiguity from the students.

The voice of the poem can produce hostile readings, as our sample student response statement in the Lexington Introduction shows. You may need to explain the dramatic voice of the poem as tentative and skeptical, since that is the condition it is exploring. It ought, however, to open up multiple readings in discussion; it is easy to respond in diverse ways to a tentative voice, since "identification" can be equally tentative.

SIR PHILIP SIDNEY, "ASTROPHIL AND STELLA, 52"

The multiplicity of a poem's audience is encoded directly into this sonnet. The poem seems to address a variety of explicit listeners and, implicitly, its readers. These include the "nymphs," presumably lady friends, who take one view, one "reading," if you like, of the situation; the speaker takes another, and the poem, perhaps, another. Then different readers, depending on their differing general repertoires, will take up yet other attitudes.

One paradoxical aspect of the sonnet form Sidney exploits is its balance between formality and idiomatic movement. The rhymes and line lengths stay strictly within the formal requirements, but unless readers are self-consciously attuned to the form (and we suggest that you don't be too overt about this), the lines flow like a conversation, producing a sense of hearing the speaking voice and thus further encouraging a sense of the poem as dialogue.

Love Poetry: Many students will find the love poetry of the sixteenth century artificial. Why, then, is it reputedly the greatest age of love poetry? Sidney, Shakespeare, Donne, Spenser, Wyatt, and some others achieved a kind of poetry that is particularly distinguished by inviting a reader's participation in a debate about love's variety--a view that is very compatible with our approach to reading generally. Try to steer discussion away from biographical interpretation. We read such poems not to find out about Sidney's or Astrophil's love affairs, but our own, to explore our own questions, issues, puzzlement, joys, disagreements. For an approach to sixteenth-century poetry in accord with the Lexington Introduction, see Gary Waller, English Poetry of the Sixteenth Century (Longman's, 1986), Chapter One.

WILLIAM SHAKESPEARE, "SONNET 8"

Reading Strategies: This poem is, of course, a classic, and many of its phrases may well seem familiar, even cliched. An initial text-centered approach is particularly valuable (with this or any other Shakespeare sonnet) since the manipulative text strategies directed towards readers are so clearly designed to be as open-ended as possible. Thus, paradoxically, as readers trace their own readings, instead of finding them "in" the text, they may rather find them in the vicinity of the text, as it were, in the way the text suggests possibilities to them. This is achieved especially by the powerfully general epithets and metaphors: we, as readers, fill in the gaps with our own particularities, as we are compelled onwards by the movement of the lines.

Love, Comparative Ideology, Sonnet Form

See the remarks on Sidney, above, and also see Waller, Sixteenth Century Poetry, Chapter Seven.

ROBERT HERRICK, "DELIGHT IN DISORDER"

A cursory reading (even, admittedly, a rereading) may produce readings that find this poem precious or "effeminate" as one of our students revealingly put it. "Sweet" is such an overused word that it takes some work to revitalize it. Such reactions shouldn't be dismissed--they can be used to mount a discussion on the ways words get over-used, especially when they carry strong social values.

Sexism: Again, a strong contemporary reading might well be one of amused indignation at the sexism. Perhaps some biography is useful, even some amateur psychoanalysis; Herrick's religion, his bachelorhood and his peculiar aesthetic sensibility have been subjects of speculation. This discussion can focus on the need for Western culture to include both "masculinist" and "feminist" components, or on the ways that, for thousands of years, men have been spoken of in sexist discourse.

JONATHAN SWIFT, "A DESCRIPTION OF A CITY SHOWER"

Title, Subject: One of our students said that "the television weatherman does this better." That remark was an interesting category mistake; what about the notion of poetry as a carefully detailed description of ordinary experience, with wit and a little wisdom, so that readers can be both amused and educated? That would be close to Swift's apprehension, yet it may not be enough for most modern readers. If that seems a widespread view, you may well get a good discussion going on changes in the social roles of poetry since the eighteenth century.

Formal Matters: Do your students prefer "formal" poetry? Is that their expectation of what all poetry is? Where do their tastes come from? Perhaps simply from schooling and a lack of adequate reading strategies to deal with other kinds of poetry. So the Swift piece may fit their expectations, and they may be able to learn the mechanical effects of the poem's formal qualities. But do they like it? Moderately, perhaps?

WALT WHITMAN, "SONG OF MYSELF" (selection)

Form, Reading Strategies: Whitman marks the beginning of the American free-verse style, where the speaking voice's breath pauses and idiomatic movement becomes the unit of poetry. It combines with a "romantic" idealization of the land, from a detailed consideration of the wonder of the grass to the nation. You can thus relate this poem to both the development of particular reading strategies and the development of a national literature. One issue some of our students have raised, however, when Whitman has been discussed as the "father" of American poetry, is that of the growing irrelevance, or marginality, of poetry. He wanted to celebrate the machine as well as the grass, of course. That may point, in some readers' minds, to the futility of poetry: the machine is self–sufficient. But such an issue has many sides, and you might encourage a discussion of the function of poetry in modern society.

Some students find it a little difficult to employ a reading strategy of simply letting the words flow. Many write poetry of their own knowing it "shouldn't" rhyme, and yet they are disappointed because it is somehow not really "classic."

ROBERT FROST, "THE ROAD NOT TAKEN"

Of all the modernist poets, Frost is probably best known. He was a well-known public figure, and his poetry has been widely anthologized for both high school and college students. Both their literary and general repertoires, therefore, are likely to be engaged by the poem—they are probably familiar with this poem, and perhaps with Frost. So you might take advantage of this familiarity by first constructing a consensual reading of the poem and then undermining it, using it to get your students to examine their own strategies for reading rather than explicating or summarizing the poem. Then philosophical questions like (2) can emerge.

LANGSTON HUGHES, "THEME FOR ENGLISH B"

Responses to the subject matter of this poem will probably be immediate. But it can also be used to bring out more interesting discussion, since it mentions some issues that frequently arise in discussions of poetry, especially the common assumption that sincerity will make something "true." Is sincerity enough? Most of your students will be skeptical about that, and perhaps find the poem naive. Perhaps, however, part of the ideology of our society encourages optimism, even naivete?

Do students' different readings of the poem depend on their racial or gender-specific repertoires? A reading might be constructed as follows: education is widely felt in our society to be a gateway to advancement, privilege, and participation in "the American dream." Is that generally true? Was it or is it true for minorities? Or for women? Could one see the voice of this poem articulating a hope that will only be rarely rewarded? Might one see the poem as showing how a minority culture should, or has chosen to, capitulate to the "literate" demands of the dominant classes?

W.H. AUDEN, "MUSEE DES BEAUX ARTS"

Auden's poetry is densely packed, and while the references to painting may make it more relevant to readers who have some knowledge of art in their repertoires, its calm, accessible texture gives it wide appeal.

Perhaps the best way to teach it is to get your students to imagine themselves in a gallery brooding over details while observing some "Old Masters." Contrast the reactions of students who have visited galleries with those who have not.

The Relevance of Poetry and Art: Art and poetry "deal with" or concern themselves with the extremes of human nature—joy, pain, achievement, horror. In what sense can poetry be said to help us understand such things? Many people have argued for the indifference of art to them—"poetry makes nothing happen," as Auden himself put it; it is "just poetry," in the words of Robert Penn Warren. Yet it might be argued that to understand such matters changes ourselves and our way of living in the world. What relevance does art have? Can it make a difference in our lives? Students will show quite different attitudes toward such questions, and Auden's poem is a useful focus for them.

THEODORE ROETHKE, "I KNEW A WOMAN"

The poem is full of sensual references and visual suggestions, such as "lovely in her bones," and "moved more ways than one." Most are not literal, but involve the reader's bringing his or her sensual associations to the lines and especially to the totality of the poem, not just to specific metaphors. Hence the overall impression of the poem is important, as is the response to metaphor. A reading strategy of trying to literalize the poem will, therefore, be confusing.

Love Poetry: Traditionally, most love poems (like this one) have been about or directed to women by men. There is both an affirmation and a parody of the role of the helpless male devotee here. You may find that many readers take it seriously, depending perhaps on their assumptions about and experience of love, but also on whether they are familiar with the tradition of putting women on a pedestal (or as one of our students put it, a "pedalstool"). Significantly, in such poetry (like the thinking that lies behind it) women, or often more accurately, women's parts, are anatomized and appraised. If students are sensitive to such issues, they may be hostile to this poem, even if they perceive it as partly mocking the convention.

DYLAN THOMAS, "DO NOT GO GENTLE INTO THAT GOOD NIGHT"

Text Strategies: The particular form of poem here is a villanelle. To follow the power created by the poem's repetitions, especially of the repeated opening line, which makes it almost ritualistic, is a good way of demonstrating the suggestive power a poem can often have for a reader. The rhymes, too, are powerful. This poem is an unusual example of how heartfelt emotion (the biographical question is relevant here) can be articulated at the same time as a concern with poetic form.

Subject: Death is a recurring subject for poetry. Students' own repertoires can be engaged to produce distinctively different readings by focusing on the question of the acceptance of death. The contrast with Donne's Sonnet 14 is a good one. Both are highly powerful poems, but take up different attitudes, as will their readers.

GWENDOLYN BROOKS, "WE REAL COOL"

Text Strategies, Ideology: Brooks's clever, cryptic poem works by its compression and wit, yet some readers may find it patronizing and aloof, with no sense of social context. Such readers will, in short, want to move from what is "in" the poem quickly to what is "not in" it. That seems a legitimate way to open discussion on the attitude of the speaker, and whether readers agree with it, and why. Some of our students have felt the poem was derisive of street kids, and some have even sensed racial overtones. Others have pointed to what they feel is compassion as well as wit. Inevitably, such readings arise from a dialogue between reader and text, in which the reading is being significantly influenced by the reader's repertoire. Don't try to force any kind of closure on the reading.

KENDRICK SMITHYMAN, "KING'S COLLEGE CHAPEL"

The role of the church in our society as a symbol of community, tradition, and human connectedness is something both Smithyman's and Larkin's poems share. Similarly, both create a persona or speaking voice that mixes admiration with skepticism. Here the emphasis is on the specific, locating the confrontation in a particular place and time, and on trying to create a different tone, more of amusement and pleasure rather than skepticism.

Is it significant that the poet is not (unlike Larkin) born in a country where superb architecture, and old cities, are found? Do your students identify themselves more with the uninvolved playfulness of this poem, or with the self-involved skepticism of the Larkin? Are there different effects of the relative indifference to theological issues here? You will probably not get readings of this poem that compare with the strong Christian reading we received of the Larkin, discussed in our sample Response Statement Assignment.

FRANK O'HARA, "THE DAY LADY DIED"

With this poem so much depends on how students are attuned to dealing with detail. Some may find it a hindrance, others a help, especially if their repertoires contain knowledge of the people and events, such as Billie Holliday herself, mentioned in the poem. You might try explicating the details, perhaps drawing parallels with other singers who have died young (Jimi Hendrix, Elvis Presley, Janis Joplin, Buddy Holly, and others). Another musical analogy some students will appreciate is the way O'Hara's poem piles up seemingly trivial, local details which cumulatively add up to a social statement--a technique that is similar to the lyrics of Morrisey, the lead singer with the rock group The Smiths.

ADRIENNE RICH, "LIVING IN SIN"

"Living in Sin" likewise deals with gender-specific characteristics, this time put in a situation that will be familiar to many of your students, even if only in fantasy!

Many students will want to read this poem literally, seeing it primarily as a descriptive text. Others, however, see the details metaphorically, pointing to the disorder and confusion of the speaker's life. A literal reading cannot easily explain the title. One issue to explore regarding the title is what exactly is "sinful." Is it the fact that the lovers are unmarried (a fairly literal reading of the title that requires a metaphorical reading of the details, since "sin" cannot simply be equated with dirt)? Other students might probe the attitude of the speaker more deeply and question whether the sinful aspect of her life is not the self-deception hinted at by the line "By evening she was back in love again."

MARGARET ATWOOD, "THIS IS A PHOTOGRAPH OF ME"

This is an excellent poem for working on reading as a process, and thus directing students' attention to their own cognitive processes. The title sets up certain expectations, which will be quite definite for many readers, centering on "photograph" and on situations in which someone is showing a friend a photo album, and saying, "This is a photograph of me when I was..." Gradually, of course, readers realize the speaker is dead. Or do your students read the "death" metaphorically? That's a crucial decision, from which quite different readings follow.

This poem is also an excellent poem for getting diverse interpretations, based on the extent to which students respond to the metaphorical level of the poem. "Where" is the speaker? How can he/she see him/herself? All kinds of different, resonant readings are possible. One interesting question is whether, on a rereading, students return and find the word "photograph" metaphorical as well. Is the "me" a person only, the soul, the "real" self? What is important is not to repress these meanings, but to help develop them as interesting and plausible readings.

Students who like to summarize or provide interpretations may well want to see the poem as "saying" something about identity, repression, self-knowledge. Others will see that as overworking it, and concentrate on the gothic quality of the atmosphere. Don't try to resolve the debate by closure—the poem opens up rather than limits meaning.

ROBERT HASS, "MEDITATION AT LAGUNITAS"

There is a long analysis of a class discussion of this poem in Chapter 5 of Reading Texts (D.C. Heath, 1987). Salient points to note are the contrast between the specificity of the lines—concentrating, in particular, on special memories, sharply focused in detail, and the general, ruminative opening. Students with some philosophical interests may relate well to the latter, especially to the issues about language and loss in the opening lines. But others may choose to focus on the images of memory.

Language: As our class discussions have shown, this is a wonderful poem for bringing into very specific focus many of the ideas about the power of language, especially those discussed in the Lexington Introduction. If language is all we have, how do we experience concrete reality? Is our culture caught between a belief in language as a neutral tool and language as a value-laden, infinitely complex system? What is the power of "blackberry"? You may look onto the Teaching Notes on the other Hass poem in the anthology for some hints on how to develop that argument.

38

GERALD COSTANZO, "DINOSAURS OF THE HOLLYWOOD DELTA"

Most students have an enormous repertoire of movie lore and myths--more, even, than they perhaps know themselves. The metaphor of seeing the screen stars of the past as "dinosaurs," remnants of a lost age, is an intriguing one, and has produced some very active discussion of the power Hollywood has in our society. You will have a variety of viewpoints--try, perhaps, to prevent the discussion from lapsing wholly into personal associations, and try to tie it together with a discussion of Hollywood and the media generally as ideological institutions of our culture.

JIM DANIELS, "AT THE POETRY READING: 'THIS IS A POEM ABOUT THAT'"

This is a fun poem that can be used in lots of ways; you can perhaps get members of a class to add examples of their own, or that they've heard at readings. The poem invites participation from readers; it is genuinely audience-centered. It is, perhaps, best appreciated by those who have heard poetry readings, especially by those poets who specialize in long introductions "explaining" their poems that are in fact often better than the poems themselves!

Anthology of Poetry

"THE SEAFARER"

Response Statement Assignments

1. This is a 20th-century translation of an 8th-century poem. What parts of the language strike you as archaic rather than modern? What effect did reading these parts have on your interpretation?

2. What do you find particularly poetic about the subject of this poem? Does it confirm or challenge your expectations about poetry?

Teaching Notes

Poetic Expectations: Many of your students may expect poetry to be more lyrical or escapist while this poem is gloomy and obsessive, a complaint rather than a celebration. You might focus on the social function of poetry, given that in our civilization it is a highly marginal activity, whereas in some societies, the poet is spokesman for the dominant values of the culture, and can be almost a religious figure. The original is a typical work of a "bardic" poet of this kind. Focus on the way that information broadens your students' repertoires.

Textual Strategies: Ezra Pound's translation given here is a loose one and you might get some interesting discussion on the way he deliberately creates mock archaisms. See "breastlock," "whale-path," and (especially) "flesh-cover" which is his translation of the Anglo-Saxon word for body. Do your students perceive the archaic atmosphere or do they see the whole poem as "Old" English? A discussion on the historical difference between cultures can grow out of this question, especially on such topics as religious consolation, life-style, and common metaphors of everyday life.

ANONYMOUS ENGLISH LYRICS: "THE THREE RAVENS"
                                    "I SING OF A MAIDEN"
                                    "I HAVE A GENTLE COCK"
                                    "WESTERN WIND"
                                    "ADAM LAY IBOUNDEN"

Response Statement Assignments

1. What parts of your literary repertoire help you to read these poems?

2. What functions does song have in your life and in the life of our society? Can you relate these poems to those functions?

3. Do you find these poems difficult or easy to follow? What reading strategies do you use to follow them?

Teaching Notes

Textual Strategies: You might want your students to relate the repetition and rhythm of these poems to what they like about the contemporary music they listen to. They might read these poems as they would read the lyrics on a record jacket, finding some of the same characteristics. Many of our students have talked about the functions that songs have in their lives: hearing them in their heads when walking; listening to music while jogging; enjoying music in leisure hours; playing the radio while on a trip. Many students will find these songs easy to follow and will understand why people respond to songs in emotional rather than intellectual ways. Some will know (and you might be able to play) one of the modern adaptations of "The Three Ravens"--for instance, the one by Peter, Paul and Mary, the 'sixties folk group.

THOMAS WYATT, "WHOSO LIST TO HUNT"

Response Statement Assignments

1. How do you respond to the dominant metaphor of hunting in the poem? What personal and cultural associations do you bring to it?

2. Consider the view of male-female relations that emerges from the poem. How is your response to the poem affected by your own gender?

3. To what contemporary situations can you adopt the final couplet of the poem?

Teaching Notes

General Repertoire (Views of Love): Like other poems of this period (this point can be extended to the selections from Raleigh, Sidney, Greville, Shakespeare and others), the attitudes to love that twentieth-century students have in their general repertoires provide a useful, contrasting way into this poem. Implied is a view of the relationship between men and women that stresses men as active (the hunter), predatory, caught between idealism and exploitation. You might get your students to study the "strong reading" of "They Flee from Me" in the Poetry Introduction and ponder the points there. The assignment and research directions there are applicable to this poem as well.

Text Strategies: Sonnets are particularly good for studying the way reading strategies develop in reaction to textual strategies in short, tightly organized poems. Traditional "information" about sonnets--the fourteen lines, the rhyme scheme, the strong couplet, the break in the Shakespearean form between octave and sextet--is useful only if it becomes part of the self-conscious creation of a reading, and leads to greater awareness of the way such text strategies contribute to a reading. "Facts" about poetic form rarely are of interest for their own sake.

Social Background (General Repertoire of the Text): The final lines are often read as Wyatt's ironical comment on his relationship with Queen Anne Boleyn, whose lover he had been before Henry VIII (Caesar) started an affair with her. You might point this out, but do not suggest that this determines the "meaning" of the poem. Instead, use it as an occasion for developing different applications ("readings") of the poem by modern readers. What other situations might your students envisage? Their own lives, even?

SIR WALTER RALEIGH, "THE NYMPH'S REPLY TO THE SHEPHERD"

--see Christopher Marlowe, "The Passionate Shepherd to His Love"

SIR WALTER RALEIGH, "AS YOU CAME FROM THE HOLY LAND"

Response Statement Assignment

What different readings can you construct for this poem? What textual strategies encourage you to see it as open-ended?

Teaching Notes

Reading Strategies: Teaching this poem can be an extraordinarily moving experience. Choose two readers to act as the lover and the pilgrim. Ask the students to decide how the lines are to be divided up between them. There will be little argument about the first seven stanzas. Then problems start--and the choices will determine the kind of reading students give to the poem. In particular, who speaks the last two words?

Consistency Building: The open-endedness of this poem can also be used to point out the crucial role of the audience, even at the time, in the making of the poem's meaning. Elizabethan poems like this would have been spoken (or sung) aloud, with the listening audiences playing a role rather like that of a theater audience. Such poems can be seen as scripts, offering different possibilities of emphasis and actively encouraging quite different readings, just as they do to modern audiences. Each reader builds up an interpretation through the emphases he or she gives the "script." The result can be (as it no doubt was at the time) an interesting debate on the poem's issues, but not a final agreed-upon, objective reading.

SIR WALTER RALEIGH, "NATURE, THAT WASHED HER HANDS IN MILK"

Response Statement Assignments

1. Imagine the poem finishing after the first four stanzas. What different view of love emerges from the shorter version? What do the next two stanzas add? And the final one? Do you find yourself using strategies to make a consistent reading of all three "parts" or do you find the contradictions acceptable?

2. What expectations are set up in your reading by the word "nature" in the title? How do they change as you read?

Teaching Notes

Literary Form: Poems are often not only <u>written</u> in layers and so adopt contradictory ideas, but they can be read as producing quite different layers of reading. Some of your students may see contradictions between the hedonism of the early stanzas and the pessimistic, even desperate cry of the final couplet. Others will use strategies that assume that interpretation involves finding unity, glossing over apparent inconsistencies, and summarizing a firm line of development. Such variations would, incidentally, have been typical of the original audience as well. "Nature" also lends itself to such a treatment: the benign deity at the start becomes untrustworthy and finally is transcended in the radical rejection of "earth and grave and dust" at the end. In both cases, the important thing here is to make the students aware of what they "naturally do" to build up meaning, rather than to focus on the meanings they produce. What you want is to get them involved in the <u>process</u> of contributing meaning, rather than of arriving at a definitive reading.

SIR PHILIP SIDNEY,   from <u>ASTROPHIL AND STELLA,</u>
     SONNETS 1, 31, 33, 45, 71

Response Statement Assignments

1. Read these poems and try to imagine yourself as the "I" of the poems. What kind of "I" do you become? What conflicts do you find yourself caught in?

2. How seriously do you take the anguish of lines 5-14 in Sonnet 1? Do you construct a serious reading of the poem or a humorous one?

3. How do your views of the relationships between men and women differ from those of the poem? Concentrate in particular on the metaphors.

4. Put yourself in the position of the woman addressed by or written about in these poems. How might you regard the speaker?

Teaching Notes

Text and Reading Strategies: Sidney's poems are especially good for stressing the way a systematic view of love and gender relations emerges from poetry, inviting readers' participation in a debate. The poems entice their readers to sympathize with Astrophil (the speaker) in his quest for Stella (the lady). It is interesting to see whether students take up negative or positive attitudes to him and whether their responses differ according to gender. Frequently our students (like those we report on in the Poetry Introduction in relation to Wyatt's "They Flee from Me") sharply divide along gender lines. The woman in these poems seems asked to be receptive yet passive, virtuous yet attractive. Women readers can easily resent such a role. "What does the <u>woman</u> say?" is a frequent response. Many years ago, one of the editors told such a questioner that it was an irrelevant question. He has repented his ignorance many times ever since!

Audience Participation: As with other Elizabethan poets, a series of audiences is assumed. The primary audience is perhaps the beloved, even though she may be entirely fictional, or highly idealized, but these poems can be adapted to various situations, including modern ones. You might consult Gary Waller, English Poetry of the Sixteenth Century (Longmans, 1986), for some further discussion of this kind of approach to the poetry of this period, most especially Chapter 1, "Reading the Poetry of the Sixteenth Century."

The Voice of the Poems: One of the reasons Sidney's poems stand out from other poetry of this period is the way he entices the readers into momentarily becoming the "I" of the poem, and so embodying a contradictory dramatic voice. Read the poems aloud to your classes--33 is especially good for its amusing, slightly melodramatic self-pity, while 45 with its sly eroticism, especially the mock tragedy of the final lines, with their erotic kick, visually provokes much laughter (you shouldn't have to explain the pun in the last line, but you never know). But concentrate perhaps on the assumption that these poems do require being read aloud: that is, until they are read and listened to by an audience, they lie inert and lifeless and, above all, emphasize that different audiences create different meanings from them. Love poetry in particular is like that--it opens up interpretation and your students should be discouraged from treating the poems as if they were paraphrasable or as if determining meaning is the most important goal.

MICHAEL DRAYTON, from IDEA, SONNET 7

Response Statement Assignment

Do you find the voice of the poem changes as you read? In particular, how do you respond to the contradictions in the poem's argument?

Teaching Notes

This is also a good poem for studying dramatic voice. Students can be asked to relate to the psychological and erotic tension, and especially to the poem's sense of audience as the argument shifts from dismissal to pleading. Do the students see it as a subtle (or not so subtle) trick? Is the poem a seduction poem? Such questions, pointing to its need for an audience, make this a poem written for reading, declaiming, performing. What difference does that make to a reader's strategies? How active are we when we listen, as opposed to when we read?

CHRISTOPHER MARLOWE, "THE PASSIONATE SHEPHERD TO HIS LOVE" and SIR WALTER RALEIGH, "THE NYMPH'S REPLY TO THE SHEPHERD"

Response Statement Assignments

1. These poems were probably written as part of a poetic debate. What issues are at stake? Can you make a contribution to the debate?

2. Did the different textual strategies—rhymes, symbols, images—of the two poems contribute significantly to your readings?

3. More generally, to what extent do you think poetry can deal adequately with such philosophical topics as love, time, aging, and fidelity?

Teaching Notes

Open-Endedness: One of the major features of reading poetry is to develop a tolerance for ambiguity or polyvalence. When we read a text poetically, we do so in order to show how it opens up different meanings in different readers—and we try to analyze the cognitive and cultural factors that produce these readings. Debate-poems like these are particularly useful for showing that reading a poem does not produce an objective, limited meaning, but instead opens up debate. Try to get your students to resist locating "themes" somehow "in" the poems—see the issues raised by the poems as occupying a relational ground between reader and text. Encourage not "the text contains/means/says..." but "the issues reading this poem brings up are..." Even "this reminds me of..." is preferable to the false kind of closure that locates fixed meanings "in" a text.

The Scope and Relevance of Poetry: Any poem can be used to bring up the issues raised in assignment #3. Poetry may seem to many students such a marginal activity that it has no relevance to our deepest concerns, to our thinking about death, aging, love, and so forth. Making us sensitive to and better able to explore such issues has been a traditional role for the poet. Who does it now? How can we use poetry? Focus on what cultural and institutional forces have given the students their repertoire of assumptions about poetry.

FULKE GREVILLE, CAELICA, 45

Response Statement Assignment

Trace your reading strategies as you focused on the changing connotation of "absence."

Teaching Notes

The Process of Reading: Greville's grim, poignant poem is useful for redirecting students' views of Elizabethan love poetry after the buoyant, witty poems of Sidney or Drayton. Try to get your students to focus on reading as a process with this poem. "Cupid's War" would be another term to focus upon: in each case, readers usually find themselves led by the nose through a series of expected associations, until the final stanza. Did any students notice (or say they did) what was going on before then? Some may find the exaggeration and idealization a bit much, perhaps.

You might want to direct your students to look at the sections dealing with connotations and metaphors in the Poetry Introduction.

MARY SIDNEY, COUNTESS OF PEMBROKE, "PSALM 51"

Response Statement Assignment

Read this poem against one of the standard Biblical translations of Psalm 51. Which do you prefer and why?

Teaching Notes

Adapting an Original: If you have religious students, you might use this versification of Psalm 51 to show how different societies and writers adapt a seemingly fixed "original." As an Elizabethan (and a Sidney), Mary Sidney turns what is in the Bible a communal song into an individual lyric, with a strong emphasis on the "I." If some (particularly religious) students are suspicious of what they might see as the insincerity of love poetry (and you may refer them to Herbert's "Jordan (I)" for some support for their case), this is a good poem to use to focus on such issues as metaphor, voice, and the matching of general repertoires.

WILLIAM SHAKESPEARE, SONNETS 29, 30, 60, 64, 65, 73, 116,   129, 130

Response Statement Assignments

1. How do you react to the view of love in Sonnets 18 and 116 (in the Reading and Responding to Poetry section)? Do you find it too idealistic? Do you find you prefer the one implied by Sonnet 129 or 130? What in your repertoire of love led you to your views?

2. Choose what you feel is a particularly striking or powerful metaphor in one of these sonnets, and show why it is important in your reading of it.

3. Typically, in Sonnet 30, lines 1–12 are a single sentence. How conscious are you of its being part of a poem? Do the lines and their rhymes matter?

4. What is the effect on your reading of the word "nothing" in line 12 of Sonnet 60? And the repetition of "When I have seen" in lines 1, 5 and 9 in Sonnet 64?

5. Trace the way your expectations change or are confirmed as you read through the first four lines of Sonnet 65.

6. At what key points in your reading of Sonnet 73 do you find yourself moving from a literal to a metaphorical reading? How is your reading changed by these points?

Teaching Notes

Interaction of Text and Reader: Shakespeare's sonnets are perhaps the greatest lyrics in the language and it would be a pity if your students did not get some sense of the awe before them that previous generations of readers have felt. But they have to approach the sonnets in their own ways. For your purposes, you might consult the notes to Stephen Booth's edition of the sonnets (revised edition, 1980), where there are some excellent hints on the way the syntax opens up meanings, or Chapter 7 in Gary Waller, <u>English</u> <u>Poetry</u> <u>of</u> <u>the</u> <u>Sixteenth</u> <u>Century</u>, where the sonnets are set in contexts highly compatible with the approach of the <u>Lexington</u> <u>Introduction</u>. Focus equally on <u>both</u> the textual strategies and the reader's involvement. There are some wonderfully persuasive uses of language here. In 29 explore the mounting climax up to the "thee" of line 10, where suddenly the poem opens up for readers to bring their own version of "thee" to bear. The opening lines of 60, with their relentless, struggling sounds, matched only by the opening eight lines of 64 or the opening of 65, are all wonderful examples of how poems can be best read when readers focus on the complex details of textual strategies.

Nevertheless, these poems are not monuments, complete in themselves: they require their readers to complete them, to <u>give</u> them meanings. So the "thee" of Sonnet 29, or the polyvalence of the narrative voice throughout, are excellent examples of how these poems invite readers in. The question of the different understandings of love, time, commitment, idealism, or disillusion--traditionally located as the "themes" of these poems--can be best focused on by analyzing the different reactions that your students will have. Some will find the views of love in 18 or 116 far too unrealistic, and they can be encouraged to construct a strong, skeptical reading of such idealism. Sonnet 129, with its lacerating sense of self-abuse, may appear, on the other hand, to be too tough to take. Sonnet 130 can be used to bring the fun back into thinking about love. When giving students the option of choosing a metaphor to follow through in their reading experiences, make it a genuine choice. It's important that there shouldn't be "preferred" choices, for the choice of a key metaphor means it is the key in the <u>reader's</u> experience. That way you can encourage the students to balance their own "ways into" the poems with the brilliant and incisive text strategies.

THOMAS CAMPION, "THERE IS A GARDEN IN HER FACE"

Response Statement Assignment

Do you find the metaphors in this poem cliches? What in your repertoire, general or literary, brings you to your opinion?

Teaching Notes

<u>Text Features: Commonplaces</u>: Perhaps bring up the question of entertainment in poetry, for with a poem like this, constructing a strong reading would seem to overload a feather! Focus on song, entertainment, lightness and relaxation, and, more important, whether students see these elements as trivial or acceptable in poetry. Like other poems of the time, this one also lends itself to examination of sexual stereotypes. Ask your students (with this or with virtually any love poem of the period) why it is that women are traditionally divided up into their physical parts--treated not simply as objects, but as objects chopped up and isolated. Do they notice? Do they find the effect objectionable? Or

does it not matter because the tone of the poem is so disarming? Does gender make a difference? Are such questions just too heavy for such a light piece?

MARY SIDNEY, LADY WROTH, "LINDAMIRA'S COMPLAINT"

Response Statement Assignment

Do you find this poem distinctive of a woman's viewpoint? Do you think there are inherently female ways of thinking and writing?

Teaching Notes

This poem might be used as part of a unit on women's writing (along with Bradstreet, Dickinson, and many of the moderns). Can students perceive anything gender-specific about this poem? The passivity, perhaps? Could they imagine a man writing this kind of thing about <u>male</u> experience? In a number of Lady's Mary Wroth's poems, she writes of how women are "molested." That's a way into a feminist reading of the whole male tradition of positioning and partitioning women in love poetry.

JOHN DONNE, "SONG: GO AND CATCH A FALLING STAR"
"WOMAN'S CONSTANCY," "THE SUN RISING"
"THE FLEA"
"ELEGY 19: TO HIS MISTRESS GOING TO BED"
"A VALEDICTION: FORBIDDING MOURNING"
"HOLY SONNET 14"

Response Statement Assignments

1. Choose one of Donne's poems and trace its argument closely. Do you find it logical? Do you find that such a summary helps you come to grips with reading the poem?

2. Do you find "The Sun Rising" or "Woman's Constancy" difficult to follow? Give detailed reasons.

3. What gaps do you have to fill in when reading "A Valediction: Forbidding Mourning"?

4. How do you read the final three stanzas of "A Valediction: Forbidding Mourning"?

5. How "modern" do you find the views of love in Donne's poems?

Teaching Notes

<u>Argument</u>: Donne's poetry is often difficult for undergraduates, which rather surprises teachers who have been educated to assume that Donne's poetry is central to our poetic tradition. With poetry of this complexity, it is often

useful to allow students to summarize the poems' arguments—so long as their responses don't stop there! Summarizing does have its uses, but only as a starting point; writing a free-association, to start to explore the personal relevances of poetry, is perhaps more useful, but again only as a starting point. However, if a student has summarizing as his or her only goal (as opposed to an initial goal), then the resulting response will probably be quite dull. After students feel they understand the poem's argument, they must change their goals and try to formulate their responses in terms of a counterargument, reading the poem against the grain.

Reading Strategies: "A Valediction: Forbidding Mourning": This is a very useful poem to help students explore the processes of filling in gaps and developing strong readings. One can pause over some of the unusual or strange words, or those "key" words that seem to be thrust out at the reader with extraordinary insistence; "melt," "sublunary," "compass," and "just" might be among the most popular choices. Whatever ways your students choose to move into the poem (there is no right way) encourage them initially to start with the argument, move into the poem's impact on them, and then begin developing a strong reading. The final lines are open to various possible and interesting readings. The poem depicts not only a dramatic speaker but also a silent character, a dramatic listener, usually read as a woman. Ask your students to think about how she might reply to the argument. Do you think she is flattered? Annoyed? Do you imagine her passively and unquestioningly, or perhaps unhappily, accepting the role she is given? There may be a hint in line 25, "If they be two..." Perhaps that suggests that the woman hasn't been at all convinced? Or that she is so convinced that the lovers are "one" that the whole notion of their being "two" is only conjecture? The way the "if" is discussed will change the reading -- it is a particularly interesting gap because the way a reader fills it will depend on what the reader has already decided the woman's response would be. See Reading Texts (D.C. Heath, 1987), Chapter 5, for an extended discussion of this poem.

Comparative Repertoires: Donne is widely admired as one of our greatest love poets. "The Flea" gives something of his wit (students may be able to bring examples of parallel situations!); "Woman's Constancy" shows something of the cynicism he explores so well, but also something of his concern with dislocation, unpredictability, and living from moment to moment, a quality students may find very "modern." If so, get them to explore not only the similarities but the differences between their apprehension of love and what emerges through the poem (a comparison, in short, of the general repertoires of text and reader).

BEN JONSON, "SONG: TO CELIA"
               "INVITING A FRIEND TO SUPPER"

Response Statement Assignment

How "sincere" do you find these poems? Is sincerity an important quality in poetry for you?

Teaching Notes

Lyrical Quality--"Song: To Celia": This is a fine poem to illustrate the song-like nature of the lyric. In fact, it's still widely sung today. If you know the musical setting perhaps you can even get the class to sing it! But some students (perhaps most) will find it rather cold and artificial. You might discuss poetry as crafted, not merely the "spontaneous overflow of powerful feelings" (Wordsworth's term).

Enjoyment--"Inviting a Friend to Supper": This is a good poem to show how poetry can evoke enjoyment, food and drink, friendship, relaxation. Get the students to reconstruct the menu for this feast and to imagine how much Jonson and his friends might have eaten! But though most of your students will find this poem to be more "sincere" than "To Celia," it too is very carefully crafted, something you need to emphasize.

ROBERT HERRICK, "TO THE VIRGINS, TO MAKE MUCH OF TIME"
"TO DAFFODILS,"
"UPON JULIA'S CLOTHES"

Response Statement Assignments

1. Outline the argument of "To the Virgins." What parts of your belief system (your personal repertoire or religious and moral ideas) are relevant to the argument?

2. Do you find "To Daffodils" sentimental, realistic, sensitive, boring? Describe and account for your response.

3. What text strategies do you find especially noteworthy in "Upon Julia's Clothes"? How do they affect your reading?

Teaching Notes

Tone and Voice: Herrick's poetry has often been seen as having a moral toughness beneath the "cute" exterior. Some of your students may bring well-developed aesthetic senses to the "Julia" poem. They will sense the text strategies that encourage the suggestiveness: the rhymes, the sensuous flowing effects of "goes," "flows," clothes," for instance. Whether they will like the effect is another matter. Some may find it (probably without being able to give the effect a name) "fetishistic."

Ideological Contradictions--"To the Virgins": is especially interesting for the way strong readings can be constructed, in this case, however, by inevitably leaving out some part of the poem. Try to encourage a Christian reading, for instance: one that would stress the religious significance of the "virgins" and the final emphasis on "marry" (as opposed to enjoyment, sensual indulgence). Then construct an irreligious or pagan reading: one that stresses the logic of the poem's argument--that it is important to indulge yourself without overriding constraints since life is short and never repeated. How do these two readings coexist? Can they? Do they in contemporary readers' lives?

GEORGE HERBERT, "THE PULLEY"
              "THE COLLAR"
              "JORDAN (I)"
              "LOVE (III)"

Response Statement Assignments

1. Read these poems of Herbert's alongside Donne's religious poems. Which do you prefer and why?

2. How effective do you find the central metaphor of "The Pulley"?

3. Describe the initial expectations set up by the title of "The Collar" and how they changed or were reinforced as you read.

4. How is the concept of love in "Love (III)" different from that of other sixteenth- or seventeenth- century poets like Sidney, Donne, or Wyatt? Which do you prefer and why?

Teaching Notes

Comparative Ideologies: Herbert's poetry is extremely good for getting students to draw on their repertoires of religious ideas and beliefs in the analysis of their experience of reading poetry. Do they find his poems didactic? subtle? Do they react more sympathetically to the quieter tone of Herbert than to Donne? Perhaps you will have some students with enough religious knowledge to identify some of the Biblical references in the poems. Such students should be encouraged to intensify their readings, just as students without extensive religious repertoires should be asked to construct "secular" readings of the poems. It's always useful to see the origins and logic of different modes of reading.

Metaphors: The poems "The Collar" and "The Pulley" carry explicit titles, which serve almost as additional lines of the poem, clearly setting up expectations. Get students to play with the different connotations they have for these words and see how far their readings are affected by them.

Argument: As with other poetry of this time, it might be useful to get the students to summarize what they perceive as the arguments before they move onto something more sophisticated, like developing their goals and strategies for constructing powerful and persuasive readings. Always stress, of course, that such summaries are useful only as starting points—and if you get distinctly different accounts of these poems, probe into what it is in the students' repertoires that has produced them. Words, especially those that are highly charged, do not have single meanings: they are always read in contexts and are inevitably multiple.

THOMAS CAREW, "MEDIOCRITY IN LOVE REJECTED"

Response Statement Assignment

How do you respond to the poem's cynicism? Would you call it "realistic" rather than "cynical"?

Teaching Notes

A good poem to insert into a debate on views about love. Do students read this poem cynically? Or without any irony? How do they account for the opening and closing lines? Does it match anything in their repertoires?

EDMUND WALLER, "GO, LOVELY ROSE"

Response Statement Assignment

Do you find the argument of this poem persuasive?

Teaching Notes

Carpe Diem Poetry: Some work on the carpe diem motif can be usefully done with this poem, Marvell's "To His Coy Mistress," and Herrick's "To the Virgins, to Make Much of Time." Pose the question to the students of whether they find the argument persuasive per se--and whether their responses are conditioned at all by their gender. We have found our male students often claim that they use similar arguments with their women friends, while the women often express skepticism about the emotionalism or macabre nature of such ideas. You might look at Kathleen McCormick's article "Theory in the Reader: Bleich, Holland and Beyond." in College English 47(1985):836-50, and also see the assignments and teaching notes on the Marvell.

JOHN MILTON, "HOW SOON HATH TIME"
"ON HIS BLINDNESS"

Response Statement Assignments

1. Contrast Milton's concern with time with that of Herrick, Marvell, and Waller. Which view is closest to yours and why?

2. Do you give "light" in "On His Blindness" a literal or a metaphorical meaning? What possible range of meanings do you perceive the word can lend itself to?

3. How do you read the final line of "On His Blindness"? How does your knowledge that the poet is blind affect your reading?

Teaching Notes

Text Strategies and Conventions: All you can do with such a brief selection from a great poet like Milton is apologize (if only to yourself!) and hope that the students will read and enjoy Paradise Lost at some point in their careers. But these two sonnets can be used to raise interesting issues. "How Soon Hath Time" can be used in conjunction with other carpe diem poems as the basis of a strong Christian reading of the originally pagan motif, and the general question of the poet's commitment to a political philosophy or to a political regime can be raised in relation to "On His Blindness." Many readers will want to sentimentalize this sonnet—you can ask what assumptions readers have about the nature of the poet and poetry if they put their emphasis on the heroic figure of the Blind Bard dedicating himself to poetry; on the other hand, if they see the poet dedicating himself to the communal interests of the state or commonwealth, what issues does that raise? How do your students understand the idea of a "committed" literature? What contemporary parallels can they find?

Didacticism and Commitment: The notion of didactic poetry can usefully surface here too. In Milton's time it was assumed that literature had moral ends. Sidney wrote that the role of poetry was to lead us to as high a perfection as our minds were capable of conceiving. But that is a view of poetry that has not been popular since the Romantics. We have had great success in giving students (without initially telling them the source) the following extract from a modern writer: "The works of authors should foster love of country and staunchness in hardship....The heroes of these works are people from different walks of life: a building team leader, a collective-farm chairman, a railway worker, an army officer, a pilot, or an eminent scientist. But in each of them the reader or the viewer sees his own thoughts and feelings, and the embodiment of the finest qualities of the national character." The writer goes on to assert that "vivid images of our contemporaries move people, prompt debates, and make people think of the present and the future."

Ask your students if this is how they think of literature. The writer is Leonid Brezhnev, the former leader of the U.S.S.R, in his Report to the 26th Congress of the Soviet Communist Party!

SIR JOHN SUCKLING,   "SONG"
                     "OUT UPON IT!"

Response Statement Assignment

How do you respond to the tone of these poems? Do you find them attractive or repulsive? Account for your response by reference to both your general repertoire and that of the poem.

Teaching Notes

Gender-Based Reading: As with other Cavalier and seventeenth-century lyrics, these poems' cynicism and masculinist (some would say "sexist" and you should explore that) tone can create an interesting contrast with the more effusive (or sophisticated) Elizabethan lyrics. Try to get your students to articulate whether they find the two different and why; they might compare, say, Sidney and Suckling with Shakespeare's Sonnets 18 or 116. Are these gender-specific differences? Do students find the Cavalier poems more realistic? It may be a question of literary or general repertoire: if students find these poems less "conventional" then it might be that these views of what literature is or should be are deeply influencing their reading patterns. Of course, these poems are no less "conventional," in style as well as in attitudes to love.

ANNE BRADSTREET, "A LETTER TO HER HUSBAND, ABSENT UPON PUBLIC EMPLOYMENT"

Response Statement Assignments

1. Do you find anything distinctively feminine (or feminist) in this poem?

2. Compare your response to this poem with that of Donne's "A Valediction: Forbidding Mourning." Which do you prefer and why?

Teaching Notes

Bradstreet as an American: Anne Bradstreet is usually regarded as the first American poet of any merit, and you might make something of that--though in this poem her status as an American is seen largely in the style in which she writes being somewhat old-fashioned. The poem, however, deals with much the same situation as Donne's "Valediction," but from the female perspective and some interesting discussion can result from comparing the two poems.

Gender-Specific Readings: See if your students develop different responses according to whose viewpoint, the woman or the man, they favor. Do you agree that the woman is essentially passive? Do they see that Mistress Bradstreet's "firmness" (to use Donne's word) in the center of her husband's travels puts her in the same role as the woman figure in Donne's poem? Students who filled in the gaps in the Donne with a vigorous, protecting woman may well be disappointed by the attitudes shown here--though they may delight in the fact that "she" does, at least, have a voice.

The question of the woman poet might get you into a discussion of woman's language--are there gender-specific words, or experiences, or are these historically conditioned rather than gender-determined? Carol Gilligan's work can be usefully referred to again--see the teaching notes on Margaret Atwood's story "Loulou."

RICHARD LOVELACE, "TO ALTHEA, FROM PRISON"

Response Statement Assignments

1. What attitudes to love, both explicit and implicit, does the poem embody?

2. How and why do <u>you</u> as a modern reader react to these attitudes?

3. What is your response to the view of sexual relationships in this poem? If you feel so inclined, construct a strong feminist reading.

Teaching Notes

<u>Developing a Strong Reading</u>: The best, most interesting, readings are those we call "strong" or "powerful"--informed, aggressive, lively and, above all, those that bring to the poem important and interesting questions and issues of the reader's own choosing. This poem has proved with our students to be a favorite for recognizing the differences between the general repertoires of text and reader.

Get your students to unravel the poem: it's a love poem, supposedly, addressed by a man, the "I" of the poem, to a woman, the "sweet" of the opening line. The poem puts forth views of love that aren't perhaps explicitly articulated, because they can be taken for granted by the poet and his assumed readers. They are the products of the dominant, shared ideology of a particular society and therefore no doubt seemed "natural" or "normal" for that initial audience. A first step in doing a strong reading is to explore some of the text's <u>implicit</u> assumptions; these can then be compared to the reader's own.

Such a reading clearly wasn't "intended" by the author. Yet most readers today would find the poem's views sexist--and even men usually have no difficulty in constructing a feminist reading.

ANDREW MARVELL,   "BERMUDAS"
                    "TO HIS COY MISTRESS"

Response Statement Assignments

1. How do you respond to the mixture of religious and natural metaphors in "Bermudas"? Do you find it surprising that they occur together?

2. "Bermudas" is concerned with the European discovery of the New World. Construct a reading of the poem that self-conscious takes into consideration something of the subsequent history of the New World.

3. How persuasive do you find the argument of "To His Coy Mistress"? Does your gender have anything to do with your response?

4. Do <u>you</u> feel the pressure of "time's winged chariot"? Is it a feeling you associate with love?

Teaching Notes

<u>Historical Context</u>: Marvell is an elegant and perplexing poet, someone whose verse opens up multiple possibilities of interpretation without seeming restriction. Even "Bermudas," tied as it is to a particular event in history, opens up issues in a quiet, sophisticated way. Don't forget that the aim of doing a reading of these poems is not to come to an objective or even agreed-on reading, but

rather to open discussion. The fear of time, the interaction of "religious" and "secular" experience, and the idealism of American history are all serious and multi-faceted issues.

Text Strategies: "To His Coy Mistress" is also an excellent poem for examining an argument in poetry. It contains a false argument: "if certain impossible conditions could be fulfilled, then I would wait for you forever. Therefore..." But these conditions are inachievable. Many of our students have seen the poem only as a seduction argument (a fairly impoverished reading, since the poem opens up far more interesting issues), but that is certainly a way into it, and you may indeed get some interesting differentiation between men and women on that. But see if they respond to the religious, scientific, and psychological issues implicit in "time's winged chariot." As ours, Marvell's age was torn between contradictory views of the universe, and those cosmic contradictions were felt, often without being easily articulated, psychologically and culturally.

JOHN DRYDEN, "A SONG FOR ST. CECILIA'S DAY"

Response Statement Assignment

Does music reveal anything of the meaning of the world? Does it put you in contact with "higher" feelings?

Teaching Notes

An interesting poem to talk about how students perceive art, music, "the arts" generally in relation to the scientific world view. Here is a poem whose repertoire includes two seemingly contradictory views of the world. It is, on the one hand, like a great composer's musical creation, with God as the composer; on the other, it is a scientific machine. Here a comparison with Marvell's "To His Coy Mistress" is useful to bring out the presence of this view. How is it that Dryden ignores the second, and that science seems excluded from his poem? This is a major absence in the poem that can be usefully explicated, especially if students themselves feel uneasily caught between conflicting world views.

THOMAS TRAHERNE, "SHADOWS IN THE WATER"

Response Statement Assignment

The poem raises the question of what the "real" world is. In your reading, did you start to interpret what the speaker sees as "real" in any sense? What in your own repertoire would reinforce this reading?

Teaching Notes

Metaphor: This is a fine poem to discuss metaphor and its relationship to "reality." It was, indeed, a question very much at issue in Traherne's time: is metaphor (and language generally) merely a way of describing the objective world, or is it a way into new knowledge? For Traherne, the latter is obviously true, yet (many readers think) it's as if the certainty of such a view is fading. Do your students find the tone of the poem wistful? nostalgic? childish? (as opposed to childlike). Many of them may well feel similarly caught between conflicting world views, and you can usefully focus on questions about metaphor and language. See, for instance, the discussion of metaphor in the Poetry Introduction.

EDWARD TAYLOR, "MEDITATION 8" "UPON A SPIDER CATCHING A FLY"

Response Statement Assignments

1. Examine the language of these poems. Do you find phrases like "God's tender bowels" or the comparison between Man and the Fly appropriate, ludicrous, effective?

2. Does it seem more natural to you to summarize these poems or to bring your own associations to them?

Teaching Notes

American Writer: After Anne Bradstreet, Edward Taylor is America's earliest poet of any merit, and you might indicate something of his isolated place in western Massachusetts, writing poetry in the vein of Donne or Herbert fifty or eighty years after them.

Text Strategies: The most useful thing to do with Taylor is probably to concentrate on the effect of his overwrought, highly moralistic style. Line 31 of "Upon a Spider Catching a Fly" is often a good place to begin--"This fray seems thus to us." Here is the starting point for that very tempting reading strategy of summarizing that many students are drawn into. With these poems you can show what is implied by such a strategy: that there is a meaning (as Taylor no doubt thought and tried to spell out), and that polyvalence is of the devil's party!

ALEXANDER POPE, "EPISTLE TO A LADY"

Response Statement Assignments

1. What is the effect of the poet's providing you with an "argument" at the beginning of the poem? Do you feel compelled to follow it through? What textual strategies reinforce that approach to the poem?

2. How "contemporary" do you find Pope's portrayal of women?

Teaching Notes

<u>Poetic Style and Reading Satire</u>: Pope's elegant, long yet economical lines may seem tedious, and his observations of women patronizing, but you might be able to use this selection to show how a poem can carry a moral argument and how it can reinforce the textual strategies: the pithy aphorisms, the punctuation of the couplet, the verse portraits, and above all (something students often have difficult with) the characteristic tone of <u>satire</u>. A useful distinction is between <u>writing</u> <u>satire</u> and <u>reading</u> <u>satirically</u>. Here Pope's point is lost unless a reader is attuned to the strategies of reading for the wit, the sense of superiority, the delight in scoring a point. If some of your students write satire for their college newspaper, you might get them to talk about why they do so. Do they, underneath, write out of indignation or a moral purpose? Or to display their wit? When they <u>read</u> satire can they admire the skill if they see themselves or something they believe in attacked? What reading strategies are involved in simultaneously admiring a satire <u>and</u> rejecting the viewpoint of the satirist?

THOMAS GRAY, "ODE: ON THE DEATH OF A FAVORITE CAT" "ELEGY WRITTEN IN A COUNTRY CHURCHYARD"

Response Statement Assignments

1. How do you respond to the lofty tone of the "Ode"? Is it appropriate to its subject?

2. Is the treatment of death and fame in the "Elegy" universally relevant? How do you, as a twentieth-century reader, respond to the social and political assumptions of the poem?

Teaching Notes

<u>Universality</u>: Gray's "Elegy" is such a standard poem in the canon that it is important to do something distinctive with it. Samuel Johnson wrote that it "abounds with images which find a mirror in every mind and with sentiments to which every bosom must return an echo." What is implied in that "must"? His remarks are a useful starting point for an examination of how ideology permeates the most ordinary experiences and assumptions, and how disagreement with such sentiments seems unnatural, inhuman. You might get your students to develop their response to the poem towards a strong reading from a position more socially aware than the one Gray occupied. Are country people always content, as Gray implies? Does he really regret the lack of ambition? Is it better to die unknown and happy? How do we reconcile such beliefs with Gray's own position as a successful and ambitious writer? How do we regard such sentiments today? Can we read the poem's sentiments as a judgement on our history? Or as sentimentality?

<u>Tone and Appropriateness</u>: The ode on the death of Gray's cat is an interesting example of how reading for the tone is important. Get students to

reconstruct the actual event--some, particularly cat-lovers, will feel sorry for the animal, and so probably will produce a reading of the poem that takes it solemnly. Others will stress the gap between the high dignity of the poem's language and the cat's death. What would the poet have said if it had been his son or daughter who drowned?

CHRISTOPHER SMART, "JUBILATE AGNO" (selection)

Response Statement Assignment

Do you enjoy this poem? Do you like cats? Do the answers to these questions relate to each other?

Teaching Notes

Another cat poem--you can comfort the cat-lovers among your students by letting them write on this exuberant, unpretentious piece. It's also a good introduction to a kind of poetry that tries to stay close to the human voice. Perhaps you can show them some Whitman for comparison.

OLIVER GOLDSMITH, "WHEN LOVELY WOMAN STOOPS TO FOLLY"

Response Statement Assignment

How appropriate do you find the conclusion of the poem? To what extent is your judgment the product of a different morality, a different era, or of your gender?

Teaching Notes

Nostalgia, Archaism: Goldsmith's little song is a charming reminder of a world we have lost--and many students will think, quite rightly. Some, however, will find it simply amusing, trivial, entertaining. Do men and women students read it very differently? What is the difference between archaism and nostalgia? Can your students be classified as having one or other of those attitudes? Or are they just healthily indifferent?

WILLIAM BLAKE,   "THE SICK ROSE"
                             "THE GARDEN OF LOVE"
                             "THE LAMB"
                             "THE LITTLE BLACK BOY"
                             "LONDON"
                             "AND DID THOSE FEET"

Response Statement Assignments

1. What ideological conflicts are there in "London"? How do you relate to the social issues in the poem?

2. How do you read the rose in "The Sick Rose" or the lamb in "The Lamb"? As you responded to the poems, did you see these in terms of a plant and an animal, or as metaphors, or as both?

3. "And Did Those Feet" is often sung as a hymn in churches. What kind of reading of the poem makes that possible? Do you agree?

4. Do you find Blake's poetry simple or simplistic? Childish or child-like? What is there in your literary repertoire about what poetry is or should be that supports your reading?

Teaching Notes

Reading Like a Child: Blake's poems are deceptively simple, and much can be made of the ways their direct language and familiar rhymes, derived often from traditional songs, open up sophisticated ideological conflicts. "London," like "The Tyger" (see the Poetry Introduction), uses words that carry and open up a rich range of meanings. The meaning of its words carry multiple significances--"ban" in stanza two is picked up by "bans" in the final stanza, thus linking "prohibition" to "marriage," and opening up a great deal of intellectual debate in the process. The multiple meanings are connotative rather than denotative, but while we bring personal feelings and associations to them, they nonetheless carry distinct social values. Another example is the name "London" itself. Like "New York" or "Los Angeles" today, it seems to stand for "the city." What do large cities represent for your students? Excitement? Power? Temptation? The connotations of "London" are, again, where ideological conflict is located. Such words are like battlegrounds, sites of struggle whose meanings battle for supremacy.

Ideology: This level of analysis shows how ideological pressures can create the poem. You can get your students to appreciate these pressures with some historical research into Blake's society. The poem articulates, as does "The Little Black Boy" more indirectly, something of the late eighteenth century's growing sense of social tension; you can talk of the terrifying poverty of late eighteenth-century Europe much in the same way as Africa's today.

The Active Reader: Note that it is the reader who builds up this reading: the poem presents gaps to be filled. From our late twentieth-century perspective, we look back and perhaps understand in more detail the complex social forces of which Blake saw only a glimpse.

Metaphor: Connotation carries values; so does any metaphorically charged language--the rose and the lamb are not just the beautiful flower and the sweet, woolly animal. They stand for human values, located precisely and historically in our culture. Do you have students who see the rose in the context of love, passion, sex, beauty in general, specific kinds of beauty? If there are students who want to literalize the poem, you can show them the kinds of reading strategies that position involves and the kinds of readings they produce, usually less interesting ones.

ROBERT BURNS, "HOLY WILLIE'S PRAYER"
"O MY LUVE'S LIKE A RED, RED ROSE"

Response Statement Assignment

What kind of humor emerges from your reading of "Holy Willie's Prayer"? What kinds of comedy are there in your repertoire that influence your reading?

Teaching Notes

You can have some great fun here, especially if you concentrate on students' expectations about poetry as literature. Reading aloud (if you can manage the Scots accent), you can convey the satiric attack on hypocrisy. Does poetry deal well with such a combination of pretty and sexy language? Perhaps some students will see the "dramatic" nature of this poetry. When teaching "O My Luve's..." try to avoid sentimental readings!

WILLIAM WORDSWORTH, "SHE DWELT AMONG THE UNTRODDEN WAYS"
"THREE YEARS SHE GREW"
"A SLUMBER DID MY SPIRIT SEAL"

Response Statement Assignments

1. All three of these poems are about Lucy, who some critics have identified with a particular woman. Do you find a literal or a metaphorical reading more satisfactory?

2. How are your expectations of what a love poem should be challenged or met in these poems?

Teaching Notes

Metaphor: These three poems are especially good for teaching students to distinguish between "literal" and "metaphorical" readings. Perhaps one reading can be done first, then another, so students can see which they prefer in order to make the poem more interesting to read. We ask them to discuss how they read the poem as it describes the speaker's feelings about the woman. Many students thought that Lucy was literally dead, though some wanted to explore what her death might signify. Others saw her death as a symbol of something/someone the poet lost in some way. What could that way be? Why in "She Dwelt..." is she so alone, why did so few people know her, why is the response of others so different from the response of the "me" in the poem? In a literal sense, she is missed only by the speaker. Why that is so then initiates a variety of comments about what she could represent. The same movement back and forth between the literal and the metaphorical exists in the other two poems though students seem to feel that "A Slumber..." must be read metaphorically because it doesn't seem to make sense otherwise. They found "Three Years She Grew" to be the most literal and many felt that the speaker was talking about a child that had died. Others noted that in stanza six, the speaker describes living with Lucy in a way that indicates her to be a lover, not a child. In the disagreement about the literal and the metaphorical, students initiate a variety of interpretations that clarify how metaphor can operate for them but also, because some students are more literal, focus on how one can respond in either way to some poems.

WIILLIAM WORDSWORTH, "I WANDERED LONELY AS A CLOUD"

Response Statement Assignments

1. How do you respond to the mood of the poet in this poem? In what way does your literary repertoire help you to understand this mood?

2. What do you think the poet expects the reader to know in order to fill in the personal gaps, especially in the last stanza?

Teaching Notes

Strong Reading: This poem can demonstrate how the language of poetry works on the emotions when one carefully reads what for many will be a familiar text. "Why is it so celebratory if the word 'lonely' is in the title?" asked one of our students. Is loneliness not a problem when one is in a beautiful spot? Is nature a cure for loneliness? Perhaps a situation like this one makes the viewer feel rich (and here we moved into the metaphorical meanings of "wealth"). Perhaps, too, the memory of the situation will provide a cure for loneliness in the future. Our students understood why their earlier experience with this poem, their literary repertoire, provided them with strategies to "enjoy" the emotional impact of the poem.

SAMUEL TAYLOR COLERIDGE, "DEJECTION: AN ODE"

Response Statement Assignments

1. What, from your own psychological repertoire, helps you to read this poem, especially as you read the first part of the second stanza?

2. What reading strategies do you employ in order to become more deeply involved with the poem? What sections do you want to reread? Why did you choose those sections? What words might you concentrate on and why?

Teaching Notes

Psychological Repertoire: Since this poem is a long and somewhat complex one for modern readers, we direct our students to look again at certain sections of the poem if they have difficulty with initial responses. "A grief without a pang..."(line 1, stanza 2) helps them to see that that the poem may be referring to a particular human state, perhaps grief, disappointment, feelings of inadaquacy, rejection, or just an ordinary depression most people have experienced. How then does the speaker describe this state? You might direct your students to see how they respond to some of the words: "stifled, drowsy, unimpassioned grief," "no relief in word, or sigh, or tear—" for example. Students may feel that while this poem contains metaphorical language, they tended, nevertheless, to respond to literal complaints such as "My genial spirits fail..."(line 1, stanza 3) because it will seem to many of them that the speaker has a serious problem of some kind. What they may disagree about is whether or not that problem consisted of a general state of mind or an actual event. "Every time the speaker gets some relief, he/she goes back into a state of misery," wrote one of our students. From such responses, you can move to a discussion of the way the poem manipulates the reader, who moves back and forth between hope and despair. Some students see the conclusion as illustrating how they often feel when worried.

We find this poem especially useful in allowing students to see how their psychological repertoires provide a way into reading the poem, with appropriate strategies. If students have read Hamlet before reading this poem, we suggest giving them a short section from the Coleridge explanation of Hamlet's procrastination so they can see the connections between his depiction of Hamlet's depression and the mood of the "Ode."

SAMUEL TAYLOR COLERIDGE, "KUBLA KHAN"

Response Statement Assignments

1. How do you use the subtitle of the poem, "vision, dream, fragment" as a strategy for reading the poem?

2. In what sense can you read this poem "literally"?

Teaching Notes

Reading Strategy: You might tell your students the story of the supposed origin of the poem, written after an opium dream, and interrupted by the arrival of "a person from Porlock," thus providing the inspiration for the Porlock Society, dedicated to the art of literary interruption and (more germane here) a long tradition of skepticism about such a story. We ask our students what it means to read this poem in a literal way; and while they may say that it helps to know something about the poem's origin or the historical figure Kubla Khan himself, nonetheless most of the reading tends to be metaphorical. While there seems to be a story, almost a kind of historical fairy tale about the vision, the fragment of a dream, the reader's response to the details and words of that dream provide the most satisfactory reading. Why is the "stately pleasure dome" located near a "sunless sea"? Why is a "deep romantic chasm" soon a "savage place"? Asking such questions points to the possibility of building different readings. Dreams, students may say, provide feelings but not necessarily sense unless thoroughly analyzed. They might see the "damsel with a dulcimer" as a major clue, perhaps as dangerous, luring the speaker into laziness and feelings of happiness which would not last. Others may apply the poem to the contemporary world, as a dream about Americans living in affluence while so much of the world is underfed. Regardless of how silly that may sound, the important thing is to probe the cognitive and cultural origins of such readings.

GEORGE GORDON, LORD BYRON, "SO WE'LL GO NO MORE A-ROVING" "SHE WALKS IN BEAUTY"

Response Statement Assignments

1. How could you bring a strong feminist reading to your response to the two poems?

2. What in your expectations of lyric poetry do you use to inform your reading of these two poems?

Teaching Notes

Feminist Reading: Here you may talk with students about the ways a contemporary feminist reading might differ from a traditional nineteenth-century reading of the poem. Then men determined the time for love as the speaker does in "So We'll Go No More A-Roving." He decides when love must have a rest just as everything wears itself out, even the sword in its sheath. Knowing that the author is a male and that the war images are masculine ones, some of our students objected to the accepted dominance of the male figure in the poem. With "She Walks in Beauty" students were even more adamant about doing a feminist reading because they objected to the stereotyped view of women in the words the poet uses: "tender," "serenely sweet," "pure dwelling place."

PERCY BYSSHE SHELLEY, "OZYMANDIAS"

Response Statement Assignments

1. The statue which this poem is written about has been described as one of the largest in Egypt. It has this inscription: "I am Ozymandias, king of kings; if anyone wishes to know what I am and where I lie, let him surpass me in some of my exploits." How does having that piece of information influence the way in which you read the poem?

2. What in your own moral or philosophical background helps you to define a reading strategy for reading the poem?

Teaching Notes

Enlarging Students' Historical Repertoires: "Ozymandias" provides a good way of having students see how knowing something about the historical inspiration for a poem, the time in which the poem was written, and then integrating those with their own repertoire, provides a strategy for reading a poem. Why did Shelley choose this decrepit statue of a great king as a subject for a poem?

Many of our students commented on the contrast between what the king says and how the statue now looks to the speaker of the poem. But what does he mean by that contrast? Is it that man is too proud? Here we sometimes ask them to research how Shelley felt about the political life of his times. What were his beliefs and attitudes? What would he have been fighting for? Many students use the information they discover to describe words like "that colossal wreck" as symbolizing more than the statue: perhaps a political figure; perhaps the aristocracy; perhaps pride in England.

PERCY BYSSHE SHELLEY, "ODE TO THE WEST WIND"

Response Statement Assignments

1. What do you think that the poet expects of you in creating the poem's images?

2. How do you read the poem in a literal way? How do you read it in a metaphorical way?

Teaching Notes

Metaphor: This poem really challenges students who try to read the poem in a literal way. Those who read it metaphorically sometimes see that the images of Section 1 of the poem tend to fall into two groups: those concerned with the leaves, and those concerned with the seeds. Some students may even note that the images of Section 2 move from cloud to storm, while in Section 3 there are two contrasting ones, the calm Mediterranean and the stormy Atlantic. What that pattern means evokes discussion of the relationship of the speaker's growth to the ways in which the images change. Does the speaker want nature to help in some way, perhaps to remove some tragedy from his life, possibly to pull him out of a state of depression, out of winter, maybe to teach him something that he does not now understand? Some students will say that the speaker finally identifies with the wind; others will see the wind as strong and powerful, everything that the speaker, while he tries to identify with nature, cannot reach. Another common view is that the images of the poem form a cyclical pattern, in which the poet attempts to relate man to the cycle of creation and destruction in nature.

JOHN KEATS, "ODE ON A GRECIAN URN"

Response Statement Assignments

1. What in your literary repertoire about the ode as a poetic form can you bring to your reading of "Ode on a Grecian Urn"?

2. How do you read the last two lines of the poem?

Teaching Notes

<u>Strong Reading and Literary Repertoire</u>: There has been much debate among critics about the last two lines of Keats's "Ode on a Grecian Urn," Centering class discussion on that debate allows students to enter into it and to discover what reading strategies help them produce the different readings they do. The poem ends with a puzzle, what deconstructive critics call an "undecidability." Is it suggesting that the ideal work of art is much better than actual life and is an image of a truth that we should try to reach, or does it bring us only a consciousness of our mortality and unhappiness?

JOHN KEATS, "LA BELLE DAME SANS MERCI"

Response Statement Assignments

1. How do you respond to the poem's treatment of love and romance? What parts of your own literary repertoire help produce your reading?

2. In what way can you respond to this poem with a strong feminist reading?

Teaching Notes

Keats's poem, some students remark, seems familiar because the situation is similar to that of many popular songs. The name--"the beautiful lady without pity"--suggests a <u>femme fatale</u>, a woman-figure who has the power to attract men to a fatal love for her. Once this is achieved, she leaves them to wander the earth lamenting their lost love. Why should these views of love remain popular? Is it that since great love cannot be sustained, it makes sense to have the lover be left? Perhaps great love is really metaphysical, like the lady in the poem, who seems supernatural, not a real figure.

<u>Feminist Reading</u>: In introducing the concept of the <u>femme fatale</u>, the poem conveys a view of women that sees them as both alluring and as possessing a power to be feared. Remind students that women were at times burnt as witches in the more superstitious days of the past. Suspicion of women's sexual powers is very common; suspicion of male sexual power is not. If students are taking classes in anthropology, get them to talk about fertility rites and menstrual taboos, about how women had been perceived as dangerous in many primitive cultures, perhaps in our own, and how women were badly treated because of male fear. Are "dominant" women still seen as dangerous because of their sexual roles and the basic control they could exert? So the "I" of the poem will continue to wander rather than to risk finding another woman--it would be too dangerous.

JOHN KEATS, "THE EVE OF ST. AGNES"

Response Statement Assignments

1. How did you respond to the narrative style of "The Eve of St. Agnes"? In what way did the strategies you used to read this poem parallel some of those used to read fiction?

2. St. Agnes was martyred about the year 300, and her feast day was important during the Middle Ages. There were special ceremonies in the church, and a legend grew up around the celebration: on the night before St. Agnes's Day a young female virgin could see, if she performed certain observances, her future husband in a dream. In a sense, this poem layers three ages: medieval, early 19th-century romantic, and your own because you are the reader. How do you respond to that layering, and how does knowing something about the historical setting of this poem, other poems written by the "romantics," and your own attitudes influence that response?

Teaching Notes

Narrative Style: This poem works well in having students see how the strategies they have developed for reading fiction can transfer directly to the reading of a poem. This kind of discussion can be used with later poems, especially the dramatic monologues of Browning. Most students follow the narrative with ease; its events, details of the setting, characters, romantic elements have many of the conventions of the fairy tale.

History and Expectations: If students enjoy the poem, focus on why they like the romance. The layering of three periods, the medieval, the romantic and their own, allows them to suspend belief while reading the poem because of their expectations about medieval castles, ladies, knights, family disputes, and daring exploits and escapes. Many of our students found themselves more engaged with the "romantics" as poets of the 19th century when those poems are set in older times. What do such reactions indicate about a reader's acquired tastes and assumptions about poetry?

JOHN KEATS, "ON FIRST LOOKING INTO CHAPMAN'S HOMER"
           "WHEN I HAVE FEARS"

Response Statement Assignment

What in your own general repertoire do you bring to a reading of these two sonnets?

Teaching Notes

General Repertoire: We direct students to look within at their own experiences as a strategy for reading these two sonnets. In the first sonnet, they recognize their own experiences when they have seen a "great" movie, or painting, heard a moving piece of music, or read a book they have loved. They see the parallels between their own exciting experience--whatever it happens to be--and the excitement of the speaker in the poem, especially because such an experience usually is short and therefore evokes an intense reaction. So, too, with "When I Have Fears..." because many of our students compared their own first experiences with death to the reactions of the speaker of the poem. The poem reflects, in form and content, the suddenness of that experience and most students have it in their own repertoires.

ELIZABETH BARRETT BROWNING, "SONNET 43"

Response Statement Assignment

Rather like the lady in "The Eve of St. Agnes," Elizabeth Barrett left her father's house, where she was treated as an invalid, to run away with and marry Robert Browning, a poet who had read her work, visited her, and then eloped with her to Italy. How do you respond to this poem once you know about the love affair and romantic marriage between Elizabeth Barrett and Robert Browning? Does biographical information of this kind exert a powerful influence over your reading?

Teaching Notes

Naturalizing the Text: Many of your students may know this sonnet but not know Barrett's background and history. There may be a (very) few students who have read The Barretts of Wimpole Street. Invariably knowledge of that background is a danger if it threatens to close off meaning, as if "background" information gave an "authentic" reading.

RALPH WALDO EMERSON, "DAYS"

Response Statement Assignment

Given the title, what immediate reading strategy do you think might help you to respond to the poem? How does that strategy work for you or change as you reread the poem?

Teaching Notes

Metaphor: Emerson's sonnet is one that demands a metaphorical reading, although students may not think so at first because of the title, which seems so literal a referent. Once students make the determination to read the sonnet figuratively, they will focus on a number of questions: What do the "daughters of time" mean to you? How can days be hypocritical? Why "dervishes" that march? What are "diadems and faggots" and how can days bring "diadems and faggots"? Ask your students to see how or whether their responses shifted at line 7, when the reader meets the speaker, the "I" of the poem. Point out, if you haven't done so yet and in preparation for the dramatic monologues of Browning, that the speaker of the poem isn't to be identified with the poet.

What does the "I" of the poem do with all of these metaphorical interpretations of "Days"? Students may comment that the speaker watches or forgets his dreams, that he may have solved his unhappiness with time and rests content with a "few herbs and apples," that he now understands that time has the better of him.

ALFRED, LORD TENNYSON, "BREAK, BREAK, BREAK" "TEARS, IDLE TEARS"

Response Statement Assignment

Both of these poems were extremely popular when Tennyson wrote them in the nineteenth century. What, in your view, accounts for that popularity?

Teaching Notes

Reading Strategies (Modern Reading): Many of our students have less than enthusiastic responses to these two lyrics so we tend to use those responses to engage them in critical discussions of why they feel as they do. Then tend to find the poems too "gushy" as one student put it, not as interesting as some of the other romantic poetry on similar themes. But some students see immediately that these poems represent a sentimental ideology of the time, just as contemporary popular lyrics have equivalent cliches. Explain that some of Tennyson's poetry was much more critical of his times, of the rise of industrialism, of the crowded cities, of the dirt and poverty in those cities. Given this, what might he be doing in these lyrics? Perhaps the days gone by and the "voice that is still" in "Break, Break, Break" refers not to a person or a personal experience but to a time when life was simpler.

ALFRED, LORD TENNYSON, "TITHONUS"

Response Statement Assignment

The note on the Greek source of the poem helps produce one kind of reading of the poem. What other kind of reading might you produce?

Teaching Notes

Multiple Strategies: This poem helps students to see that sometimes a small amount of background information can enlarge their repertoire and help them develop a reading of a text. After reading the note explaining the story of Tithonus' struggle with eternal life but not eternal youth, students can easily construct the gist of the poem. How might another way of interacting with the poem be developed? The drama of the situation--the misery, the illness, the constant desires that cannot be fulfilled, the boredom, the hopelessness--can be generalized to broader contexts. The dramatic monologue form (as with Browning and Eliot) makes the poem more like a script than a "personal" revelation--perhaps some of the students will be reminded of Hamlet's soliloquies.

ALFRED, LORD TENNYSON, "ULYSSES"

Response Statement Assignment

How does the dramatic monologue form influence your reading?

Teaching Notes

Some students might ask why this form suddenly seemed to become so popular: talk about the decline in the writing of plays at the time when Tennyson and Browning were writing--perhaps the dramatic monologue served as a substitute, perhaps it has something to do with the reification of inner experiences, with the characteristic Romantic/Victorian dualism of "inner" and "outer" realities.

If students see Ulysses as an old man looking back to the glory of his former life (a few students may remember Ulysses from reading The Odyssey), they may be able to construct a reading about old age in general--the poem might sound very much like some older people they knew, people who wanted to tell them about their past and who tended to repeat. What might confuse students is deciding where the poet stands in all of this. Some of them feel that the reader can believe the last lines, "To strive, to seek, to find, and not to yield," while others see these lines as ironic, as typical of someone who is fooling himself. Focus on why it is that such lines are undecidable--is it part of the formal nature of the poem, or a product of what readers bring to it?

ROBERT BROWNING, "MY LAST DUCHESS"

Response Statement Assignment

Write a response to this poem that presents a strong reading, either feminist or political.

Teaching Notes

Feminist and Political Readings: Here clearly the dramatic aspect of the monologue can be stressed, with the poet almost a member of his audience, listening in. Students may read the poem as a comment on how women were treated at the time, as objects to be owned like slaves, especially by members of the aristocracy. One student insisted that the listener and the Count below are just as bad as the Duke. A political reading of the poem therefore becomes possible by addressing attention to the power and privilege of the aristocracy: the Duke could kill, talk about it, and marry again. Students felt strongly that although Browning's poem is written about an older society, it nonetheless reflected his thoughts about his own.

WALT WHITMAN, "I SAW IN LOUISIANA A LIVE-OAK GROWING" "THE DALLIANCE OF THE EAGLES"

Response Statement Assignment

What in your literary repertoire can you use in order to read these poems? What makes them poems? What do you focus on? How do you respond to these kinds of poems?

Teaching Notes

"I Saw in Louisiana a Live-Oak Growing" may appeal to the environmentalists! The speaker in the poem sees the live-oak and wonders how it can be so joyous when it has no friend nearby. The speaker knows that he could not be joyful in such a situation so he takes the twig to his room to think further about the tree. He realizes that it makes him think of friends, of how much he misses them, of how important loving other people is to him. Again, students may see the poem as talking, in simple and straightforward language, about the importance of each human being, and the importance of love. Some may note the emphasis on "manly" love and question that, in which case the question of homoeroticism can be introduced. Others may see that more generally.

WALT WHITMAN, "OUT OF THE CRADLE ENDLESSLY ROCKING"

Response Statement Assignments

1. In what way do your own beliefs about love help you to read this poem?

2. In what way does the title provide you with a strategy for reading the poem?

Teaching Notes

Ideas of Love: We use this poem so that students will see that love in Whitman's sense extends to all things, although he uses the image of one kind of love in order to speak about love in a broader sense. You may find that reading parts of this poem in class helps students, because they can then pay more attention to the repetition in lines like those that start with "From" or "And" in the first part of the poem.

"I could see this poem as a folk song," said one of our students and we tell them that Whitman has been popular with folk singers, that some of his poems have been put to music. The question about love usually emerges again as we ask students if they think that Whitman is talking about a great romantic love in his example of the bird that loses its mate. Most of them feel that Whitman ties in the bird with the boy's realization of the love of all things in life and in death. Others commented that the poem had to do with the love of all things in nature, with both joys and disasters, with the cradle endlessly rocking from the time one is born until one dies. The speaker of the poem learns, then speaks directly to the reader through the eyes of the boy, the longing of the bird, the sun, the dark, all of the nature images.

WALT WHITMAN, "A NOISELESS PATIENT SPIDER"

Response Statement Assignment

What are the consequences of reading this poem literally? Metaphorically?

Metaphor: We ask our students if they can read this poem either way, and they see that it can be read literally or metaphorically. They see that the line, "And you O my soul where you stand," can tie up the literal and the metaphorical, that is, that the soul operates with its body in the way that the spider interacts with its web.

WALT WHITMAN, "CAVALRY CROSSING A FORD"

Response Statement Assignment

Construct a strong political reading of this poem.

Teaching Notes

Political Reading: Students tend to react strongly to this poem, either liking it or hating it. And they see that what they feel depends on their own political reactions to the military. Those students who viewed the military positively liked the poem; the anti-militaristic students may be cynical about descriptions of military flags that "flutter gayly in the wind." We talk with our students about the Civil War, about Whitman's attitudes toward slavery, about his not being willing to fight but his willingness to work with the wounded, about his position as a pacifist, and how such contradictory views might possibly be held together.

MATTHEW ARNOLD, "DOVER BEACH"

Response Statement Assignment

Consider the advantages and disadvantages of a strong feminist, political, or religious reading of this poem.

Teaching Notes

Multiple Readings: At times it seems a good idea to provide three possible options so students can see how to make different kinds of choices because of what they bring to their reading of the text. Many students have read this poem in high school and have already formulated some responses to it. Most generally can at least summarize it. Students who have read the poem before or who have information about Victorian England tend to come up with a political reading. A feminist perspective is also fairly easily produced. Students would see "Dover Beach" as a love poem from poet to lover, and one that, some will think, given its time, has nothing objectionable in it. What it implies--that the world is difficult, "the grating roar," paralleling the human misery, cannot be changed. But the love of a man and a woman, of any two people for each other, can help if the two can be true to each other. Are such sentiments acceptable today ? (See Hecht's parody "Dover Bitch" for one view of this!)

Students can also try a religious reading. Although "the Sea of Faith" is difficult to hear in a modern world, is it still there? Perhaps it stands for all of what constitutes spiritual love in a secular and difficult world? Or else it may signify the waning of one of the Western world's central beliefs--the belief in God--the loss of which the nineteenth century felt especially keenly.

MATTHEW ARNOLD, "TO MARGUERITE"

Response Statement Assignment

How do you use your literary repertoire to respond to this poem?

Teaching Notes

Literary Repertoire: We use this poem after we have introduced students to other Romantic poets, such as Shelley and Keats, and they tend to recognize that it fits into that tradition. But they might see that the poem has built-in differences because although it is about a love, a lost love probably, it seems to go beyond that. On a literal level, the poet talks about the separation between England and France, the mainland of Europe, suggesting that God is responsible for that separation. But on this level, one might sarcastically ask why the speaker cannot, like most people, simply cross the Channel in a boat. So there's immediately a possibility of another, metaphorical, level: that these separations are political; that one person from England, probably a man since the poet is male, cannot love a woman from the other side of the channel because of cultural differences; that the man is of one class, the woman of another; that each made a decision to separate but the speaker continues to regret his decision; that the speaker regrets not being able to live on the continent; that for psychological reasons, he sees the sea as estranging. You might compare this poem with Wordsworth's Lucy poems for further speculation.

EMILY DICKINSON,   POEMS 67, 214, 303, 449, 465, 585, 712, 986, 1052

Response Statement Assignments

1. In reading the Emily Dickinson poems, notice the short, terse style of the lyric as compared with any of the poems you have read by Wordsworth, Keats or Shelley. What readings of these poems do you create when you try to fill in their "gaps"?

2. In what way do you respond to the language of these poems?

3. Emily Dickinson is one of the few women of her time whose poetry is now considered to be part of the canon. Her poetry, until recently, was not considered to be feminist. How do you think a feminist reading works with these poems?

Teaching Notes

Gaps: We generally find that reading some of the Dickinson poems in class helps students to become involved in what is often a difficult kind of reading for them. The elliptical nature of the Dickinson poems tends to be confusing unless students immediately understand they they can fill in gaps from their general repertoires. "A narrow Fellow" is perhaps the most obvious: lines like "His notice sudden is," may be chosen by students who note the inverted line and say that although the poet may literally be talking about a snake, its connotations are multiple.   Fear of snakes is a common one, the fear of encountering one can be immediately generalized to a fear of anything sudden or unexpected. If students relate the snake to the Garden of Eden, then it can connote a general fear of evil. If read as a phallic symbol, it suggests a fear of sex.   Said one student, "We all have irrational fears of walking into a dark house when we're alone at night." Some students saw this latter observation as a fear of rape common to women and noted that this speaker/poet is a woman. We also discuss gaps as they emerge from the way in which the speaker communicates to the reader, in phrases where one part of the phrase can contradict the next, as in "Burst agonized and clear" where the word "agonized" seems as if it should be something more like "happy."

Multiple Readings: Irony and Ambiguity: Many students will read these poems ironically, and some will note a deeper and tragic sense that works along with the irony. Others will see playfulness and humor. We read some of the poems in class to see why we perceive them in different ways.   Many of the poems seem to combine contradictory moods, even the tragic with the comic as in the line in which death "kindly stopped for me."   This tragic line is somewhat humorous (albeit black humor) since death does not "kindly" do anything. "But it can be kind if you are in terrible pain," said one student, while others disagreed and said that the word had to be ironic, perhaps reflecting an irony that pervades the whole of our existence. We cannot control death; it stops for us, as Dickinson says, whether we want it to or not. Students perceived that the soul is treated with irony in the way that it selects its own society, then closes "the Valves of her attention" as if a soul can literally do that. Many students saw this poetry as revealing how little power the individual has over what cannot be controlled in life; therefore the poet laughs, cries, satirizes, comes to terms with, accepts, hates this aspect of reality. One student commented that a woman in Dickinson's time would feel especially vulnerable. That comment leads to a discussion of a strong feminist reading of the poems as another way of informing the ambiguities.

Feminist Reading: Here is where we find the most exciting discussion of Emily Dickinson. You might ask your students to do some research on criticism of her work. It is frequently argued that she is really an "androgynous" poet, that her work goes beyond her gender in her greatness as a writer. Modern feminist critics would see that view as naive. You might therefore ask students why previously so few critics discussed her poetry as feminist. One student reported on an essay in which Dickinson's work, along with the work of a few other women, is seen as feminine because of its terseness: women had to be careful what they said.

Some of our students saw "I like to see it lap the Miles--" as a subtle reference to sexuality and read the metaphors in that way. Others felt that although "I taste a liquor never brewed" seemed on first reading to refer to nature, it could also refer to female sexual needs. While there was some disagreement as to the validity of bringing a feminist reading to these poems, many students agreed that "I never saw a moor," could be read not only as religious but also as a pleading, though subtly, for a freedom the poet/speaker does not have but can imagine.

CHRISTINA ROSSETTI, "SONG"
               "REMEMBER"

Response Statement Assignment

Here are two poems by another Victorian woman, though in many ways a non-traditional woman for her time in her sense of freedom about sex and other aspects of her way of life. Both of these poems share the elegiac approach to love and loss that you have encountered in other of the Romantic and Victorian poets. Can you think of anything in your repertoire that informs your reading of this poem so that you respond to it differently from the poems by men? Do you think that your response has anything to do with your gender?

Teaching Notes

Gender-Specific Response: These two short poems provide a way of looking at gender-specific responses, although it may take a little time to elicit such responses from students because they are not always sure at first why they respond as they do. If students have read Dickinson, then they know that her style is so different from that of the male poets they have read that she cannot be compared to them in the same way that Rossetti can. Rossetti's style is very much like that of Shelley, Keats, and others, but somehow the content differs. Some might consider that although she is English, and Dickinson American, they seem to have something in common. What that can be is a kind of mood, yet many find it difficult to explain what that mood is. Telling students about the significance of Rossetti's association with the pre-Raphaelite movement helps them to understand her. They may not easily see any affinity with Dickinson. The feeling of martyrdom in the poems might be a connection. There is a morbid note in her telling the person she addresses in the poem that they shouldn't feel guilty if they forget her for a while, "For if the darkness and corruption leave...Better by far you should forget and smile." Somehow this trait of martyrdom seemed more feminine than masculine to many of our students. Such arguments can spawn discussion about whether women are "intrinsically" more masochistic than men, whether they are socialized to be such, and whether women today think they still are.

LEWIS CARROLL, "JABBERWOCKY"

Response Statement Assignment

How does either your literary repertoire or your interest in language influence the reading strategies you use to respond to this poem?

Teaching Notes

Literary Repertoire and Interest in Language: This poem is often read by one of mutually exclusive sets of reading strategies. First, students can read the poem as a satire of a world in which people talk in riddles, in a language that makes no sense to them or to Alice. Some students enjoy talking about the political and social satire of the speaker who warns of the "Jabberwock," representing a Victorian moral code, a social situation, a war. The words aren't supposed to make sense. If the poem is not read as a satire, however, but as a kind of puzzle, students try to make the text cohere into something meaningful. This is a fun assignment, since students' attempts to translate nonsense words into real words suggest the arbitrary nature of language and the strong role of the reader in developing interpretations.

THOMAS HARDY, "NEUTRAL TONES"

Response Statement Assignments

1. How does your reading of other texts by Hardy inform your reading of this poem?

2. How do your attitudes to gender affect your reading of this poem?

Teaching Notes

Intertextuality and Feminist Reading: Many students may have read a Hardy novel in high school, and we ask them to compare the heroine of that novel, or the love relationships, with what they read in the poem. Some of them will respond that the woman does seem like others of Hardy's women; she is not romantic and pure but rather someone of "tedious riddles" coming from her past. Perhaps this is not her fault, but she is nonetheless dangerous, since her smile is so much a "deadest thing/Alive enough to have strength to die." One line that readers may ponder over, especially those who have read Hardy, is "that love deceives." This line provides a clue to some students who see the dead quality of the woman as not her fault but rather as resulting from a conflict between the lovers and the "love" ideology of the culture.

THOMAS HARDY, "CHANNEL FIRING"
"DRUMMER HODGE"
"THE MAN HE KILLED"

Response Statement Assignment

What strategy do you find most useful to read these poems? In what way can you use a political strategy in the sense that all three poems contradict a dominant ideology?

Teaching Notes

Dominant Ideology and Political Irony: Living in the late twentieth century, we have all experienced, directly or indirectly, the horrors of war, genocide, invasion, the appropriation of huge proportions of national wealth for "defense," and so forth. Of course, students will have varied attitudes on these issues. It's often argued that many of the militaristic ideas of our age, especially in Europe, originated in the nineteenth century. As with Conrad's Heart of Darkness (which many students will have read), Hardy's poem frequently meditates on the destructiveness of Victorian society. You might discuss the extreme patriotism of Victorian society and of the doctrine of manifest destiny, that the white man had a duty to spread his culture to more primitive people. Beneath the pious surface, of course, was England's role as a powerful nation controlling and exploiting other people for economic reasons. In "Channel Firing," we discuss the wars between England and parts of Europe, the guns across the Channel, the fact that God sees the activity as "gunnery practice out at sea"--almost a funny image when juxtaposed with death and the simple but important question "Will the world ever saner be...In our indifferent century." Is the century indifferent to the death of its young men who fight? Similarly Drummer Hodge, the ordinary soldier, dies for ambiguous reasons and will lie, not at home, but where "strange-eyed constellations reign/His stars eternally." Why he dies is unclear as are the reasons for the war. The man of "The Man He Killed" would have rather met the enemy he does not know at "some old ancient inn" where they could have been friends. Our students find these three poems easy to read, but they disagree on whether the poems are unpatriotic or humane.

THOMAS HARDY, "AH, ARE YOU DIGGING ON MY GRAVE?"

Response Statement Assignment

In what way do your expectations about how you are perceived by those who love you help you to respond to this poem?

Teaching Notes

Reader Expectations: Our students initially laugh at this Hardy poem until we ask them how they would feel if they died and no one really cared, not even the dog. Some see the poem as perhaps too cynical. Others disagreed and felt that people should not take themselves so seriously, that no one can be constantly missed. Some students point out that Hardy might have been laughing at the reader expectations of the time--sentimentality, as in Dickens or in some of the other poetry they had read about all-consuming grief. Others said that the poem had contemporary meaning because we all have expectations that we will be missed a great deal, and the poem challenges those expectations. Some of our students discussed their childhood fantasies of death when they were angry at their parents. "I liked to pretend I died, so they would miss me and be sorry," one student wrote.

GERARD MANLEY HOPKINS, "THE WINDHOVER"

Response Statement Assignments

1. What, in your view, does the windhover represent? Or do you read it literally?

2. How does the style of this poem compare with other nineteenth-century poetry, for example, by Wordsworth or Rossetti?

Teaching Notes

Literary Repertoire: You might use this poem to illustrate how the romantic lyric can change both its form and its content. Reading the poem in class, students can see that the lines run over, that words are arranged elliptically and do not flow as students probably think they naturally should. Note the alliteration and the packing of images one on another.

The significance of the windhover is clearly religious, yet most students will argue that the poem is more confusing than traditional hymns.

GERARD MANLEY HOPKINS, "GOD'S GRANDEUR"
"PIED BEAUTY"

Teaching Notes

Literary and Religious Repertoire and the Use of Metaphor: We find that providing our students with some background material helps them to follow Hopkins as a writer of the meditative lyric, because it is difficult to place him chronologically. While all his poetry was written during the Victorian period, it did not reach the public until around 1918 when he became something of a cult figure for those turning back to religion as well as those interested in non-traditional poetic forms. Our students often see Hopkins' work as unusual, and it must have seemed even more so when he wrote it and when it first became popular. Some students, especially those involved in religious activities, suggested that Hopkins had to write in an unusual mode because he was writing against his times when science became, in a sense, a new religion. Some may point to the poem's metaphors as related to God's creation of and connection with man in very sensual ways. Those students who were less religious related these images to sexuality, and you might discuss the relationships between sexual and religious images, a current issue in Hopkins criticism. To continue this discussion, it might be useful to compare Hopkins' poetry with the religious poetry of Donne and Herbert.

A.E. HOUSMAN, "LOVELIEST OF TREES, THE CHERRY NOW"

Response Statement Assignment

How do your own age and expectations about growing old influence your response to this poem?

Teaching Notes

Matching of Repertoires: This poem, in some ways, resembles the carpe diem
poems.   Students who have read and liked them immediately go straight into
summarizing this poem for a "message":   make use of every moment because
one is constantly aging.   Some students talked about their grandparents' wishes
that they had taken better advantage of their youth.   Some of our students felt
that one can't possibly make use of every moment, so Housman may be being
ironic, as with the wonderful and funny counting in the second stanza and the
ambiguous line about the "cherry hung with snow."   Other students may see
religious symbolism in the cherry tree: in fact most of the metaphors are
traditional ones, and if you give your students the selection of medieval lyrics to
read alongside it, they may make some parallels.   All of these readings
presuppose, of course, a metaphorical reading, ignoring the literal level.   What if
students read the poem as simply about a cherry tree?

W.B. YEATS, "A PRAYER FOR MY DAUGHTER"
"LEDA AND THE SWAN"
"WHEN YOU ARE OLD"

Response Statement Assignment

In these poems Yeats writes about relationships, and various kinds of love.
How would you characterize the view of human relationships they evoke?   Do
you agree or disagree?

Teaching Notes

"A Prayer for My Daughter" serves as a good way to have students respond
to what, in a sense, constitutes fatherly advice--the kind of life and personality
that the speaker wants for his daughter. Maybe some of your students will
respond that perhaps Yeats is writing satirically, that he can't possibly want
these things for anyone: beauty, but not enough to make a man's "eye
distraught," with not a handsome but a wise man for her husband.   And what
about, "In courtesy I'd have her chiefly learned"?   He wants her to be merry,
content to live in one place, and be quiet, hating "intellectual hatred" which "is
the worst," secure in a house where ceremony is important "for the rich born."
Some of our students insist that he can't be serious.   Others respond by seeing
him as completely serious and argue that, for his time, he might be describing a
happy life for a certain kind of woman.   Perhaps you might suggest that the
poem is oversimplified if it is seen as being about a daughter at all--perhaps it
is more interestingly read as being about the speaker's picture of the kind of
security a woman can have.

"When You Are Old" provokes discussion if some students see the poem as
sexist while others see it as dealing with love that lasts beyond superficial
beauty.   Many may feel that the notion of loving beyond superficial beauty is
itself patronizing and sexist--what she is to dream of is "the soft look...Your

eyes had once..." One student said, "Would a woman tell a man to look back on his soft look?" Students also tried to place the "pilgrim soul" in the context of how they felt about the poem. Was it wandering, religious, and political, as Maude Gonne was in Yeats's life? (You might tell them about his relationship with the activist Irish actress.)

The central metaphor of "Leda and the Swan" can bring strong reactions. Many students will dislike the male power, the female "helpless breast upon his breast." One student wondered if Yeats was, in fact, questioning his own picture of male power in the last two lines of the poem, especially in the question, "Did she put on his knowledge with his power..." and the possibly implicit criticism in the description of "the indifferent beak...." Try to encourage wider cultural readings—seeing the poem as indicative of a brute, mindless power that many see as distinctive of our century.

W.B. YEATS, "AMONG SCHOOL CHILDREN"

Response Statement Assignment

This poem is the most famous, popular poem that Yeats ever wrote. The last two lines of the poem are quoted as much as many of the lines in Shakespeare or the end of Keats's "Grecian Urn." How do you read these lines? What possible alternative readings might be made?

Teaching Notes

Literary Repertoire: This poem, which depends in its later stanzas on esoteric allusions and mystical and philosophical concepts, is sometimes difficult for our students to follow. The problem of a sixty-year-old man contemplating his own past, however, makes sense to them as they think about their parents' and grandparents' nostalgic and often meditative musings about the past. You might suggest they compare this to Robert Penn Warren's poems which appear later in the Lexington Introduction. Perhaps it is useful to expand the students' repertoire by explaining images: the allusions to Leda's body and Plato's parable of the caves; scenes that the speaker recalls (9-12), the speaker's beloved; "pretty plumage" and "old scarecrow" (lines 29-32); the significance of the word "mother" (37); "the self-born mockers of man's enterprise" (56); "Labour is blossoming or dancing" (57-60); and of course, the last two lines, the dancer and the dance. Explaining such references shouldn't be designed to produce an objective, agreed-on reading, but rather should open students up to the possibility of multiple readings.

The dilemma posed in those last two lines and the way in which the poet leads up to them make up a classic example of polyvalence. One of our students, a dance major, suggested the following: "A dance is a joyous pattern of movement with a rhythmic relationship to a work of music. The dancer is the being who engages in this pattern of movement. You can't have one without the other. What Yeats says to me is that it does not pay to make pointless distinctions since I, at least, can find what I look for in a kind of unity of everything around me, even in growing older." Other students, as we continue to look at the poem carefully, suggest that readers respond to the tensions in the poem, the oppositions that the speaker sets up: the love of the mother and the love of the nun; beauty vs. scarecrow ugliness; and they agree that all these contribute simultaneously to human conflict and the need for oneness.

ROBERT FROST, "MENDING WALL"

Response Statement Assignment

How does your work with theory in this course influence your reading of a poem that you have read and discussed before?

Teaching Notes

Literary Repertoire: Most students will have read "Mending Wall" in high school since it appears in nearly every high school anthology. Thus we find it a good poem to use to explore how their new reading strategies and theoretical assumptions and practices influence their readings of poems with which they are familiar. Most students also know something about Robert Frost and his role in American literature, especially that of New England. What they say initially is that "Mending Wall" concerns a man who, unlike his neighbor, wishes that walls were not necessary to keep peace among people, in this case two persons, in a larger sense, groups. They also discuss the informal tone of the speaker as he relates to the reader in a kind of dialect. But rather than stopping with a summary, as they might have in high school, they can now be encouraged to read the poem on multiple levels: to look for contradictions in the argument of the speaker; to explore the ideological assumptions underlying the poem's argument; to explore ways in which these might (or might not) be seen as distinctively American; to compare self-consciously the general repertoire of the poem with their own general repertoire.

ROBERT FROST, "BIRCHES"
"STOPPING BY WOODS ON A SNOWY EVENING"

Response Statement Assignment

How do you respond to the mixture of seriousness, irony, and ambiguity in these poems? What kind of a strong reading helps you to enjoy what may superficially seem to be simple and clear? Is there something about the denotative and connotative meanings of the words in these poems that helps you to read them with more understanding?

Teaching Notes

The Narrative Style: While our students have read dramatic monologues, they respond in a different way to Frost's poems until we suggest that they try to read them as they would read fiction. What is the narrative style? How does that style involve you in the poem? What are the elements of that style? What constitutes narrative and its effects? They respond with answers like the following: the "I" in each of these poems tells a story; there are other characters; the narrative seems as if it could be part of a story rather than a whole story; each poem ends with an ambiguous idea, one that has to be pondered. As for poetry, they see not only the denotative aspects of words, but also their connotative nature—the metaphors, the poetic form, and the many descriptive phrases. How do these integrate? Many students like Frost because his poems simultaneously tell a story, but refuse to put closure on that story. Frost asks questions that he does not answer: why could one "do worse than be a swinger of birches"; what does it mean to have "miles to go before I sleep"; can we ever know which decisions are best—or is the road less traveled always the best? Students had many comments on these poems and their responses to them: Is the road less traveled by the road that is most difficult? Must man be as busy as the speaker who stops by the woods? What does one get in remembering and returning to one's youth?

WALLACE STEVENS, "THE EMPEROR OF ICE-CREAM"
                  "ANECDOTE OF THE JAR"
                  "THIRTEEN WAYS OF LOOKING AT A
                  BLACKBIRD"

Response Statement Assignments

1. Is "Thirteen Ways..." really about blackbirds? Is "The Emperor of Ice Cream" really about ice cream? If you see them as about something else, what reading strategies are you using to construct that reading?

2. Wallace Stevens spoke of poetry as the "supreme fiction" by which we live, a means of achieving a sense of order in the world. As the reader, do you respond to his poetry in any way akin to that? Do you find that his poems create a world of their own? Or are they a commentary on the world?

Teaching Notes

For students with an aversion to poetry, Stevens's poems are often allusive, tedious, seemingly too "aesthetic." You can get them to develop such initial reactions into an analysis of their expectations about poetry and their strategies, especially whether they naturally read poetry for a "literal" or "metaphorical" meaning. Do they see "Thirteen Ways" as having a message of "pay attention to physical things" or an invitation to play with language? Try to substitute something else for "blackbird"—does the poem work as well? Is it the message or the sensation that matters? Is poetry trivial if it just invites us to enjoy a series of discrete sensations?

WILLIAM CARLOS WILLIAMS, "THIS IS JUST TO SAY"
"THE RED WHEELBARROW"

Response Statement Assignments

1. If you found "This Is Just to Say" as a note on the refrigerator, not written out as a poem, would you interpret it any differently?

2. What makes "The Red Wheelbarrow" a poem?

Teaching Notes

Williams actually claimed this poem was a <u>note</u> he'd written to his wife. She probably read it <u>monovalently</u>, for its information content, not its "poetical" nature. Poetry is as much a way of reading as a way of writing: we have experimented with our classes by giving them lines from the instruction pages of the telephone book, arranging them in short lines on the page, telling them that it is a poem and asking them for their interpretations. Inevitably, all kinds of poetic devices are <u>found</u> in the poem—symbolism, allusion to other poems, rich connotations. It "all depends" as Williams himself put it, on the perspective of the reader.

Williams was called "anti-poetic" by Wallace Stevens—and you might ask your students to contrast the two poets from the selections given here. For Williams's style of poetry, what seems to matter is to take ordinary language and make us read it intensely, "poetically."

EZRA POUND, "IN A STATION OF THE METRO"

Response Statement Assignment

What kind of relationship do you find between the two lines? What is the basis of your answer? Visual? Intellectual? Connotative?

Teaching Notes

Pound's little "image" (he was, when he wrote this, a leading supporter of "imagism," a movement to create poems as detailed, unified, and concentrated images) is an excellent focus for getting students to say what this kind of poetry consists of—a way of reading ordinary words with an eye to concentrated effect.

MARIANNE MOORE, "THE FISH"
"POETRY"

Response Statement Assignments

1. What reading strategies do you use in reading "The Fish"?

2. Do you agree that poetry is "useful"? In what sense?

Teaching Notes

The most common strategy for reading Moore's poetry is probably, initially, to read to get the gist: the text strategies slow down a reader, suggesting that an argument is being asserted. When you get to a phrase like "literalists of the imagination" then that strategy may become a problem. Is the imaginary the literal? Perhaps this is a line that the consistent "literalists" in your class will blur or ignore. That's an interesting reading habit to focus on.

T.S. ELIOT, "RHAPSODY ON A WINDY NIGHT"
"THE LOVE SONG OF J. ALFRED PRUFROCK"
"GERONTION"

Response Statement Assignments

1. Do you find Eliot's poetry difficult to read? If so, why? What strategies do you adopt to deal with the difficulties?

2. Do you see the male figure in "Gerontion" or "Prufrock" as typical of the modern world, as many readers argue?

3. What does old age signify to you in these poems?

Teaching Notes

Eliot's fame as a poet, combined with his notorious difficulty (odd as that appears to teachers well trained in New Criticism, of which Eliot was a Founding Father), can easily alienate students. His work may appear ponderous and over-learned. A good initial strategy is perhaps to see the poems as dramatic monologues in the tradition of Browning, Tennyson, or Burns, and also as playing out internal dramas. Thus, the typicality--the dislocation of the modern world, the uncertainty, even the sense of self-delusion and doubt--can also be seen as the characteristics of an individual. Do your students go straight to this level of typicality? A common reaction to Eliot's poetry (as to a great deal of modern literature) is that it is depressing, pessimistic. Concentrate a little perhaps on the dramatic humor, the elements of caricature, if you can get your students attuned to the way the poem can be "produced" like a play.

The old age emphasis in Eliot is again open to multiple interpretation. Don't force a "typical" reading of old age upon your students; they may relate more easily to a less allegorical reading.

E.E. CUMMINGS,   "MY SWEET OLD ETCETERA"
                    "SOMEWHERE I HAVE NEVER TRAVELLED,
                    GLADLY BEYOND"
                    "O SWEET SPONTANEOUS"
                    ,"SHE BEING BRAND"

Response Statement Assignments

1. How do you respond to Cummings's syntax, punctuation, and arrangement of lines?

2. "Etcetera" is an obvious "gap": how do you go about filling it? By the end of the poem, how have your initial expectations derived from the title changed?

3. Trace the way your reading of "she being Brand" changes as you move through the poem.

Teaching Notes

Cummings's jaunty, idiosyncratic writing is often a great starting point for a unit on the sheer enjoyment of poetry. Even if you can't work out the exact reason for all the syntactical and punctuation oddities, the overall effect is usually great fun. The naivete and spontaneity the poems celebrate, echoed in the textual strategies, and the language Cummings invents can be fun to decipher, but more fun just to let flow. These poems can become less searches for meaning than a process of experience, with words moving readers on to discover the surprises and fun of manipulating language.

Ensure that you don't force your students to find a single, shared meaning for the unraveling of any of these poems. Part of the fun of Cummings is the different surprises that emerge in different readings.

COUNTEE CULLEN, "YET DO I MARVEL"

Response Statement Assignment

In your reading, how did you fit the final line into the poem's argument? How does your own ethnic background affect your reading?

Teaching Notes

This is an interesting poem to show how poetry articulates more than just "literary" values. You can broaden the discussion into the ways our society has marginalized certain groups, how they have used "high cultural" forms (like the sonnet here) to try to work their way into a less peripheral position. You might as well ask why a twentieth-century poet would use a sonnet, itself a fairly archaic form, to articulate such sentiments. Cullen's poetry was denigrated in the 1960s by militant black writers who found it lacked social awareness; perhaps this poem calls that into question. Do your students agree? Do their distinctive repertoires as students of the latter part of our century make a difference?

EARLE BIRNEY, "FOR GEORGE LAMMING"

Response Statement Assignment

Try to summarize this poem. Do you think the experience of reading a poem with a voice so like the speaking (or thinking) voice allows you to produce any useful generalizations?

Teaching Notes

One of the predominant characteristics of much contemporary poetry is an approximation of the direct personal voice. Here the poem's voice is that of a poet looking back to an event with some friends and articulating a worry (as such poetry often does) about the clumsiness of language—its inability to embody our deepest feelings. Paradoxically, the scene with the images of black and white, flowers and face, can evoke some moving and personal observations by other readers. You might focus discussion on that issue. Perhaps you will have in class some students who write such poetry themselves and can talk about some of their writing strategies.

RICHARD EBERHART, "THE FURY OF AERIAL BOMBARDMENT"

Response Statement Assignment

What is your response to the difference between the language in the final stanza and that of the first three?

Teaching Notes

The technical language and the names of the final stanza can produce a real shiver down the backbone. The slightly melodramatic early stanzas, built around a series of grim, unanswerable questions, come down to the list of names and (for most readers, as no doubt for the military recruits themselves initially) incomprehensible technical terms.

Some students may find the descent bathetic and boring. That provides a useful opportunity for examining the different reading strategies and different repertoires of the readers (for instance, on the subjects of war or of God).

KENNETH REXROTH, "PROUST'S MADELEINE"

Response Statement Assignment

Does the association of the memory of the speaker's father with the poker chip seem arbitrary to you?

Teaching Notes

You might point out the origins of the title—a very personal childhood memory recorded by Proust that brings back rich feelings to him as an adult. This is another poem that conveys the impression of the speaking/thinking voice. Part of the effectiveness of the poem, at least to most readers, is its apparent arbitrariness. Do you think students feel rather dissociated from the particular associations? How do they relate to such a direct address from the poem's speaker? Are they tempted to summarize or to make personal associations? Can you get them to move from their personal responses into some analysis of their cultural assumptions? What picture of America does the poem evoke for them?

ROBERT PENN WARREN, "SMALL ETERNITY"
                     "RUMOR VERIFIED"
                     "YOU SORT OLD LETTERS"

Response Statement Assignments

1. What expectations are set up by that paradox in the title, "Small Eternity"? Trace how your expectations are confirmed or altered as you read.

2. The relationship between the past, recalled in memory, and the present is crucial in all these poems. How does your own sense of that issue interact with the poem? Does your repertoire overlap with the text's?

Teaching Notes

All these poems use the narrative voice of an older person looking back. They were, in fact, all written late in Robert Penn Warren's career, in the 1980s. That may provide your students not with "the" meaning, but with a particular perspective to wrestle with. Your students are mostly, presumably, young persons without the long, fading, or distorting memories that are displayed in these poems. How do they react? Do they find these poems scary? Irrelevant? Do their reactions stem from their youth or from their broader world outlooks? Can they see themselves taking up attitudes like those articulated in the poems?

W.H. AUDEN, "LULLABY"

Response Statement Assignment

Read the poem aloud and try to account for the effect of the rhythm on your reading.

Teaching Notes

Most readers will read this with heavily end–stopped lines, and this poem, unusual among twentieth–century poems, benefits from such reading. It has the effect, often, of a song without the formality of a song's rhymes. See what kinds of reactions you get from your class. Do they find it reassuring, thus taking the title literally?

THEODORE ROETHKE, "DOLOR"
"MY PAPA'S WALTZ"

Response Statement Assignments

1. Do you find the pencils sad in the contexts that the poem describes? What is the effect of choosing the settings in which the pencils are found?

2. How would you characterize the tone of "My Papa's Waltz"? Happy? Nostalgic? Angry? Disillusioned? Romantic? Explore some of the ways in which your repertoire intersects or clashes with the poem's. Do you think the speaker had a happy childhood? Do you think he thinks he did? What role does the mother play in this poem? Explore her role in relation to larger cultural issues of feminism and motherhood.

Teaching Notes

Roethke's attention to detail—the buttons on the father's shirt, the minute details of "Dolor," can produce comedy, nostalgia, and a strong division of responses into hope and humor, gloom and despair. You will probably find that students bring many personal associations to these poems—the very concentration of detail demands that, and the intersection of poem's and reader's repertoires may well produce varied reactions. A strong anti-dolorous reading of "Dolor" is a possibility, since the poem may well be read as a celebration of ordinary detail, not a record of sadness.

DOROTHY LIVESAY, "THE UNQUIET BED"

Response Statement Assignment

How do you read the word "men" in stanza 3? Construct a strong feminist reading of this poem.

Teaching Notes

Whether or not Livesay was aware of the irony of "men" in stanza 3 is beside the point. The poem can open up various kinds of feminist reading: a concentration on roles (stanza 1), inheritance (stanza 2), and a desire for power (stanza 4) as well as the ambiguous and undesirable (stanza 3).

ELIZABETH BISHOP, "THE FISH"
"VARICK STREET"
LETTER TO N.Y."

Response Statement Assignment

How do you respond to the personal voice in poetry? Do you feel the poet is talking to you? Or do you prefer something more distant, seemingly "objective"?

Teaching Notes

Both the New York poems are interesting for their cool control of form, with the dramatic, ironical little song, and the mock-letter, a kind of conversation in verse. "Letter to N.Y." rhymes quite formally (abcb for the most part), yet it works best when read informally, as though it really were a letter. Do the students respond to that mixture? Do they like the rhymes? Does the combination work? What roles do their expectations about poetry play in their answers? With "The Fish," you can no doubt get lots of personal associations brought into the poem. Do your students share the moral conclusions Bishop builds in? What parts of their general repertoires make the "lessons" or "morals" they draw different?

KENNETH PATCHEN, "DO THE DEAD KNOW WHAT TIME IT IS?"

Response Statement Assignment

How do you interpret the poem's last line?

Teaching Notes

This is a wonderful poem for reconstructing a dramatic situation and developing multiple readings. Get your students to focus on both the contrasts and the interconnections between the two stories. Then see how differently they construct the poem to make that last line fit. Who is speaking? How does the title fit? In dealing with the last line, don't aim for closure or a final, agreed reading. Let variety reign!

IRVING LAYTON, "THE BULL CALF"
"KEINE LAZAROVITCH 1870-1959"
"BERRY PICKING"

Response Statement Assignment

Birth, love, and death are among the great shared realities of existence. Can poetry help us deal with them?

Teaching Notes

Layton's highly emotional (some would say moving, some melodramatic) poems make good foci for students concerns—or lack of concerns!—with poetry's power to present or help deal with these so-called "unusual" experiences. Some students will relate very closely to the experiences in these poems: the slaughter of the calf, the death of a parent, feelings about love and nature. The issues to focus on are probably less the personal associations than the extent to which poetry can or should try to "deal with" such experiences. What is it to "deal with" death? Do we want comfort, understanding, compensation? Can poetry give us any of these?

DELMORE SCHWARTZ, "THE HEAVY BEAR WHO GOES WITH ME"

Response Statement Assignment

At what point did you start to read this poem metaphorically as well as literally? What in your literary and/or general repertoire helps you read it metaphorically?

Teaching Notes

You can get students to describe the bear's traits, but many will want to move straight to the metaphorical level, an indication of which may be picked up in the title. Does the poem produce optimistic or pessimistic readings? You might even try to get the students to critique the kind of body/mind dualism that runs through the poem (as well as a great deal of Western thinking, perhaps to its detriment).

JOHN BERRYMAN,   "A PROFESSOR'S SONG"
"THE DREAM SONGS 4, 14, 375"

Response Statement Assignments

1. What do you think is "the law against Henry" (Song 4)?

2. Do you read the dog in "Dream Song 14" literally or metaphorically?

Teaching Notes

Berryman's poems, with their wry self-deprecation, are excellent for getting students involved in reading poetry as contributors to an on-going conversation. In Song 4, they can take parts, interpreting "Henry" and "Mr Bones" in terms of their own views on love, responsibility, restraint, politeness—and, of course, the relationship between fantasy and "reality." Perhaps they even sense that the fantasy level, the internal brooding, is more "real." Perhaps Henry's worst offense is that he explores in his fantasy what a polite, civilized inner world excludes.

Once again, metaphor is an important way of thinking in these poems, not just a way of "expressing" a pre-existent truth, but a way in which readers can enter into a text, defining and exploring their own experiences as they unravel it. Rereading is important for exploring metaphor as well; you often realize that your reading was being formed much earlier than you thought.

RANDALL JARRELL, "A GIRL IN A LIBRARY"

Response Statement Assignment

What might the girl's reponse to the (presumably male) observer be if she knew what he was thinking?

Teaching Notes

Point out how traditionally love poems are written by males looking at women who are often unaware that they are being so objectified. Does the description, which some of your students will, we expect, find sentimental and patronizing rather than affectionate or moving, reflect this situation?

DYLAN THOMAS, "THE FORCE THAT THROUGH THE GREEN FUSE DRIVES THE FLOWER" "FERN HILL"

Response Statement Assignments

1. How do you respond to the metaphorical language of "The Force..."? Do you find it confusing or stimulating?

2. Do you have in your own memory a place like Fern Hill? What is its significance for you? How does it influence your reading of Thomas's poem?

Teaching Notes

"The Force..." is a poem that repays careful reading aloud to get the bardic timbre, the insistent rhythms, the use of paradoxical and contradictory imagery. Some students will find it too loud, too melodramatic and insistent upon sound and suggestion, insufficiently close to the ordinary speaking voice. Perhaps it's closer to the speaking voice of an inebriated Welshman? Someone drunk on words? What is the force that unites all these elemental feelings? Breath ("wind")? Love? Polarities?

Fern Hill was a country house that Thomas visited frequently as a child, a piece of biographical information that may help locate the experience of the poem. The last lines may be usefully glossed, not to establish their meaning, but to enable readers to find analogies and then generalize to see the cognitive and cultural dimensions of the experience. Do they suggest that time is the great enemy holding us in chains (compare some of Shakespeare's sonnets)? Or is this how poetry and creative genius generally act: operating within rules yet exploding beyond them?

ROBERT LOWELL, "TO SPEAK OF WOE THAT IS IN MARRIAGE" "FOR THE UNION DEAD"

Response Statement Assignments

1. How do you respond to the voice of "To Speak of Woe"? What might the speaker's husband's version of the relationship be? How does your own experience influence your reading?

2. How do your own feelings and beliefs about the history of America

influence your present actions? Apply your thoughts on that subject to your reading of "For the Union Dead."

Teaching Notes

Lowell's poems are often difficult to teach students, and the temptation is always to fall back on biographical reductionism, noting his Puritan/patrician New England ancestry, his years of Catholicism, his role as a conscientious objector, and so on. These two poems can be seen more as dramatic monologues. Even "For the Union Dead," although a personal meditative poem in Lowell's confessional-autobiographical vein, fastens onto something sharable and concrete: episodes in American history to which readers can relate. Try to focus on the interaction of the observer's voice and public events in these two poems, as they consider marriage and the pressures upon men and women, couples and contradictory events of our history, distant and recent. Get the students to bring their own equivalent experiences to bear on their readings; then the "I" of the poem can become a much more shared one.

AL PURDY, "SONG OF THE IMPERMANENT HUSBAND"

Response Statement Assignment

Give an account of the other side of this argument--provide the wife's voice.

Teaching Notes

A comic reply to Lowell's "To Speak of Woe," perhaps? In this poem, the subject is made into a joke, but the restlessness is still there. More significantly for teaching the poem, students can perhaps be asked why the male speaker of this poem can joke about such a situation, whereas the female "I" of the Lowell poem cannot. In discussion, make sure such answers draw on the cultural repertoires of the students. In addition to their "personal" views, the status of women in traditional marriages is clearly relevant.

LAWRENCE FERLINGHETTI,   "IN GOYA'S GREATEST SCENES WE SEEM TO SEE" "UNDERWEAR"

Response Statement Assignment

Do you find Ferlinghetti's conversational style appropriate for comedy and satire?

Teaching Notes

Students who prefer the direct-voice style of poetry should relate easily to these poems, especially when read aloud. "This is poetry...?!" is a common response to "Underwear," meant as a compliment or an expression of relief. In particular, it is a poem that is useful for starting off a unit of poetry to show its power of immediate enjoyment and vivacity. You might have the students read our discussion of Jim Daniels's "Short-Order Cook" to emphasize the point.

HOWARD NEMEROV, "THE GOOSE FISH"

Response Statement Assignment

Do you interpret the lovemaking of the lovers as the central event of the poem, or just a convenient starting point?

Teaching Notes

This is a fine poem, rich and complex in its suggestiveness, for showing how metaphor can open up personal and cultural significances. It starts out seemingly as a love poem, with a romantic setting and physical passion, and then suddenly seems disrupted by the fish. A comment on love? Don't try to get agreement or closure. Focus instead on the different readings the poem makes possible, even readings that change as the poem moves on, and how those readings are devised. Are students' own experiences, personal or literary, directing their interpretations? Or do they think it is "in" the text?

RICHARD WILBUR, "THE WRITER"

Response Statement Assignment

Which of the father's two wishes for his daughter do you prefer? What advantages do you suggest the writer might have?

Teaching Notes

This poem provides a nice, simple structure—two situations juxtaposed to show how a complex metaphor can work. The question isn't easily answered, despite the speaker's developing awareness of what he sees as his just and loving wish. Both alternatives have their advantages. Even if the second is more "realistic" (not to mention, as many of our students point out, in tune with the common American ideological insistence that struggle and difficulty make achievements worthwhile), ought a "wish" perhaps to be aimed as high as possible? Is that ideological as well?

PHILIP LARKIN,   "AN ARUNDEL TOMB"
                 "THE WHITSUN WEDDINGS"

Response Statement Assignments

1. Do you agree with the two "almosts" in line 41 of "An Arundel Tomb"? Give your reasons for taking the position you do. If you disagree, do you think they spoil the poem?

2. As you read "The Whitsun Weddings," do you find your interest or identification moving between the speaker and what he is looking at? What points are especially crucial in the development of your reading?

Teaching Notes

Larkin's meditative, ironic poems are--as we explained with "Church Going," in the Reading and Responding to Poetry section, often surprisingly suggestive. However quiet, they are subtle and perceptive. Some readers will be overcome by the atmosphere of nostalgia or romantic idealism that "An Arundel Tomb" can produce and not notice the "almosts." When that qualification is pointed out, an important question becomes how they relate it to the rest of the poem. Is it prefigured? Do they reject its apparent negativism? Do they find it realistic? Expectations about their own lives and love experiences may deeply influence their readings.

The power of "The Whitsun Weddings" is similarly devious. Try to capture a dramatic sense of the speaker--have your students ever been in a situation where they watched others' un-selfconscious behaviors and found their observations disturbing? Some will find the tone throughout a peacefully celebratory one; others will find the whole scene disquieting and threatening. Try to probe why, not just on the "subjective" associative level, but on the level of culturally produced beliefs and assumptions, about such matters as love, hope, and ritual.

ANTHONY HECHT,   "THE DOVER BITCH: A CRITICISM OF LIFE"

Response Statement Assignment

Do you find Hecht's poem a fair "reading" of Arnold's "Dover Beach"?

Teaching Notes

You can get a great deal of fun from this poem, both in itself and, most especially, in its amusing "reading" of Arnold's solemn "Dover Beach." An interesting issue, however, is whether the poem is an enjoyable jeu d'esprit or a revelation of some of the attitudes implicit (though perhaps not acknowledged) in Arnold's poem. Read in such a manner, Hecht's poem can be seen as a twentieth-century commentary, not just on Arnold's poem, but on whole aspects of Victorian attitudes to sex, relationships, religion, and gender-relations. Thus it is an excellent example of a multiple comparison of both general and literary repertoires.

CAROLYN KIZER, "AFTERNOON HAPPINESS"

Response Statement Assignment

Is happiness a "poetic" subject? Is is possible to write memorably or profoundly about joy?

Teaching Notes

What a great poem to challenge so much of our culture's puritanical assumptions about the seemingly necessary connection of profundity, tragedy, pain, and insight! You can point out the falsity of the common assumption that the really "poetic" subjects are always anguished, as well as focus on the view that poets are somehow supposed to write best out of deprivation or misery. Here is a fine poem that clearly disproves that! Do your students (especially those who write poetry themselves) agree or disagree?

KENNETH KOCH, "MENDING SUMP"

Response Statement Assignment

Do you read Koch's poem as a tribute to or an attack on Robert Frost's style of poetry (see "Mending Wall")?

Teaching Notes

Parody is often double-edged; Koch's amusing poem parodies the grimness and emotional sparseness of Frost. But to what extent does he reveal the narrowness of Frost's poem while still admiring his taut verse? You'll doubtless get differing arguments on this, which may well derive from preference and assumptions about poetry (literary repertoire) as well as views of the world (general repertoire).

MIKE DOYLE, "GROWING A BEARD"

Response Statement Assignment

What is "poetic" about this poem? Are there poetic strategies "in" the text that may help you?

Teaching Notes

This is an amusing little poem, quietly observing a common event yet with a witty turn of phrase. It is conversational, yet its precisely chosen, ordinary language is neatly crafted. Does that seem "poetic" to your students? What assumptions do they have about what poetry should be?

ROBERT CREELEY,   "I KNOW A MAN"
                  "IF YOU"
                  "THE WAY"

Response Statement Assignment

Do you find these poems playful or serious?   Which predominates in your reading?   Which do you prefer and why?

Teaching Notes

Creeley's poetry is very interesting and often immediately appealing—a mixture of intense, direct emotional experience, often painful or threatening, with a very sparse, controlled line.   There is a "metaphysical" quality that some of your students will bring out in their readings.   The wit and quiet grace of Creeley's lines point up some interesting insights; their simplicity provides a stimulus for readers to draw on their own repertoires to fill in the details.

A.R. AMMONS,   "AUTO MOBILE"

Response Statement Assignment

Is this poem about a car?   Or about a person?   Or both?   Comment on the strategies you use to construct your reading.

Teaching Notes

Clearly, the poem is more fun if it's seen as being about a lover, wife, husband even, but it still works well on the "literal" level.   But you might focus on whether both readings aren't metaphorical.   After all, to call a car "madam," however conventional, is still to employ a metaphor!

FRANK O'HARA,   "WHY I AM NOT A PAINTER"

Teaching Notes

Like O'Hara's Billie Holliday poem, the issue of personal detail in each can be used to focus on the way in which the merely personal might be seen as a barrier to readers.   Some students will write poetry themselves and perhaps will have faced the question of "authentic" detail from their own experiences: what difference does it make if "this really happened."   Whether it makes good poetry is the question that can be asked.   Most educated readers would say yes to these, but some will find the details trivial and pointless.   As usual, the key issue is the assumptions behind such readings, not whether they are right or wrong.

JOHN ASHBERY, "AND UT PICTURA POESIS IS HER NAME"
"DECOY"
"CRAZY WEATHER"

Response Statement Assignment

Do these poems make sense? Do you find them difficult to read? What reading strategies might you use to provide a coherent reading of them? Is developing a coherent reading a desirable goal?

Teaching Notes

There is no doubt that Ashbery's elliptical, sophisticated, and complex verse is difficult. His lines work not by normal syntactical rules, but primarily by absurd surrealistic associations and conceits. Often going on seemingly in a very commonsensical, even humdrum, voice, it will then move violently and unpredictably onto another subject.

Many of your students may find that music or painting provide useful ways into these poems. "It's almost as if he doesn't want the poem to mean something," one of our students paradoxically put it. Various conventional reading strategies can work in part, but summarizing often merely frustrates, and while free associating will work well, it often leaves most of the poem behind. To search for connection seems to mean that meanings proliferate, tumbling over one another. Allow students to play at length with the multiple meanings of a word, a line, a section of the poem. Many students will try to thematize or summarize, which is acceptable as long as they see how inadequate that strategy is to the experience of some of Ashbery's lines. From reading Ashbery's poetry, some students will begin to recognize the pleasure of reading a text that does not cohere. Such an experience can provide almost endless interpretive possibilities as ideas are combined and recombined. Encourage students to revel in the poem's linguistic virtuosity.

ROBERT KROETSCH, "MILE ZERO"

Response Statement Assignment

What strategies do you use to deal with the fragmentary nature of this poem?

Teaching Notes

Kroetsch's poem is a "post-modern" piece stressing fragmentation and decenteredness. It seems to regard poetry as a search, not a formal unity. Will your students be puzzled by such writing and find it too obscure? In fact, there is a simple linear structure they could use, one given by the poem: each fragment is a night in a journey, presumably from east to west. But the fragmentation of experience, too, has certain recurring possibilities for readers preferring to stress narrative in their readings: the different kinds of poetic experience encountered, different imaginative experiences, the ambiguity between the world as literal and the world as metaphorical. What is "Mile Zero," i.e., where do you start (or end)?

PHILIP LEVINE, "THEY FEED THEY LION"

Response Statement Assignment

What is the effect of the rhythms of the poems? What parts of your literary or general repertoires influence your reading?

Teaching Notes

Read the poem aloud, stressing the rhythm. Do your students have chanting in their backgrounds? Hymns? Political slogans? Any kind of religious ritual? Those are useful areas to draw upon to produce a powerful emotional experience in reading this poem.

ADRIENNE RICH, "A CLOCK IN THE SQUARE"
"AUNT JENNIFER'S TIGERS"

Response Statement Assignments

1. Do you read "Aunt Jennifer" as a comment on women in our society in general? Or on women poets?

2. What do you think an anti-feminist reading of Rich's poetry would be like?

Teaching Notes

Rich's superbly articulated feminism emerges even in her early, rather tentative poem, "Aunt Jennifer's Tigers." Later she herself looked back at the poem as a strong reader, noting what she saw as a "split" between "the girl who wrote poems, who defined herself in writing poems, and the girl who was to define herself by her relationship with men." Does such biographical information reinforce a "biographical" reading, or point to a wider aspect of cultural history, especially of the women's movement? Do your students note how the pride, confidence, and fearlessness of the tigers are paraded as "masculine" traits? Is this true to their experiences? "Ringed" is, of course, a key word in the poem.

TED HUGHES, "CROW'S FIRST LESSON"
"CROW'S THEOLOGY"
"THE THOUGHT-FOX"

Response Statement Assignments

1. What connections exist between the fox and the speaker in "The Thought-Fox"?

2. How do you respond to the "theology" of the two "Crow" poems?

Teaching Notes

Hughes's tough-minded poetry in the "Crow" poems is perhaps at first contrastable with the metaphor of the fox in "The Thought-Fox," but the same toughness is evident: the analogy between a poet and a fox is an unusual one. The poem shows two realities, the poet in the lighted room, his own forest, and the fox in the dark forest outside. Does it upset or even amuse your students to have the poetic imagination (supposedly a high and noble attribute) likened to "a sudden sharp hot stink of fox."

The Crow poems may also provoke some religious discussion. These poems are compressed, intense myths of the creation of Love and the nature of evil in the universe. Perhaps get your students to outline the orthodox stories on which they are based. Then discuss the power of the myths in relation to the poems, and (especially) what it is in their religious repertoires that produces their particular readings.

GARY SNYDER, "LOOKING AT PICTURES TO BE PUT AWAY" "MARIN-AN"

Response Statement Assignment

Do you think these brief lyrics make significant comments on our society? What in your assumptions about poetry (literary repertoire) and society (general repertoire) influences your reading?

Teaching Notes

Snyder writes compact, sometimes cryptic, and evocative poems, often with a surprisingly obvious moral attached. Students attuned to contrasting inner and outer realities and especially to seeing poetry as being able to bring out our apparent awareness of such dualities as man and nature, inner and outer, sexual and mechanical, will relate easily to him. Others may find him boring, obvious, too "sixties" in feeling.

SYLVIA PLATH, "THE APPLICANT" "TULIPS" "MORNING SONG"

Response Statement Assignment

How do you respond to the intensity of these poems? Do you think they reflect a particular personality or are more universal?

Teaching Notes

Plath's intense, somewhat neurotic and self-concentrated, confessional poetry works differently on readers. Some readers will find it unhealthy and threatening; they may think that even a "song" written by a mother to her baby becomes self-obsessed, with the child seen as an inhuman object of horror and fear. The flowers in the hospital become threatening, and the view of marriage obsessive, destructive, and negative. But others, especially some of the younger women students, among whom Plath sometimes remains a cult figure, will see the poems as intense, perceptive, capable of evoking "their" feelings. The poems provide an opportunity to open up the question, as with Rich and Lowell, of the problem of "confessional" poetry. Can it be at once "true" to the poet's experiences and "universal" or "relevant"?

ALDEN NOWLAN, "THE MYSTERIOUS NAKED MAN"

Response Statement Assignment

What is the "meaning" of the man in the poem? What in your literary or general repertoires helps to produce that reading?

Teaching Notes

You can easily focus on the open-endedness of metaphor with this poem. Maybe, too, there will be "literalists" in your class, readers who will say a naked man is a naked man and nothing more. Certainly the poem stands up just fine to such a reading. Others may want to produce a heavy allegorical reading—is the man a scapegoat, a victim, our "essential selves"? And so forth.

LEONARD COHEN, "UNTITLED POEM"

Response Statement Assignment

How do you respond to the last line of the poem in relation to the rest?

Teaching Notes

A slightly melodramatic poem that many students will respond to as if it were a literal record of a remembered love affairs, until the last line. Some will pick up the clues in both the title (a parody on the common practice of not giving titles to poems or paintings) or the first line. Focus on the different reading strategies that produce these different readings.

MARGE PIERCY, "BARBIE DOLL"

Response Statement Assignment

Do you find this poem effective as feminist writing? To what extent do your own gender and literary repertoires influence your reading?

Teaching Notes

Some students, even those with feminist inclinations, will find this poem unsubtle. Perhaps, some may argue, it wouldn't have been ten years ago, but there are many persuasive writers who work the same theme better. Such a comment is perhaps more influenced by literary than general repertoire. Perhaps a useful comparison might be with Plath's "Daddy," which is also an angry, even strident, statement, but much more evocative and open-ended.

ROGER MCGOUGH,   "MY BUSCONDUCTOR"
                       "AT LUNCHTIME: A STORY OF LOVE"

Response Statement Assignment

Are these "serious" poems? Comment on the mixture of comic and serious.

Teaching Notes

McGough was a member of the 1960–70's rock group The Scaffold (which had a number one hit, "Lily the Pink" in the late sixties), a piece of trivia that you may find it useful to know if there's an amateur popular music archivist in the class.

The poems are often useful for introducing "fun" poetry to a recalcitrant class, and then showing how such light poems can also be "saying something" about the human condition. They're not subtle poems, but they can provide good discussion on the way poetry works.

JAY MEEK, "THE WEEK THE DIRIGIBLE CAME"

Response Statement Assignment

What do you think the dirigible stands for?

Teaching Notes

An excellent poem for showing the open-ended nature of symbolism. Let your students make as many different suggestions as possible. Don't attempt closure. Some students will even want to see religious parallels in the mention of the days. If you have access to Donald Barthelme's short story "The Balloon," about a huge balloon that settles over Manhattan, some useful parallels can be made.

JOHN NEWLOVE, "CRAZY RIEL"

Response Statement Assignment

What relationship do you find between the first twenty-five lines and the rest of the poem?

Teaching Notes

In this poem, we watch how thoughts grow into a poem, especially through the interaction of the restless contemplative mind with a seemingly stable, mythical figure from the past. Riel was both a man of action and a rebel. The poet today may often seem to be a rebel, but how much action is he responsible for? Students will take up different views of the poem's development, but if they simply summarize it, it will lose any significant impact; a merely associative approach may end up being trivial. If, however, you can get personal associations moving towards some larger, more sharable issues, then more interesting readings may result.

ISHMAEL REED, "BEWARE: DO NOT READ THIS POEM"

Response Statement Assignment

What limits are there to the subject matter of poetry?

Teaching Notes

An excellent poem for the first day of class discussion on poetry. It directly addresses many students' fears about poetry, and by literalizing them, makes them laugh at themselves. A good poem, especially when read (or chanted) aloud, for showing how the details of everyday life can be fused together into a poem. Does that make it a good poem? What effect does poetry have in the world? Is it possible to share the particular details the poem presents? The poem is also making a number of rather subtle points about the power of language. Gently introduce students to these. But by and large, let them revel in the humor of the poem and in the recognition that they have information in their general and literary repertoires that are relevant to reading this poem.

MARGARET ATWOOD, "THE ANIMALS IN THAT COUNTRY"
"YOU FIT INTO ME"

Response Statement Assignments

1. What are the advantages and disadvantages of the two worlds in "The Animals in That Country"?

2. Outline a feminist and a masculinist reading of "You Fit into Me."

Teaching Notes

Atwood's austere, powerful poems will usually produce excellent discussion that can, hopefully, avoid paraphrase and trivial free-associating.

Readers' Repertoires: The world of art or fantasy is contrasted with the world of "reality"—but which is more real? You should get a variety of emphases in discussion of "The Animals." Students will see both the perfection or harmony of art and the actuality yet imperfection of the harsh "real" world. Some may bring references to the Judeo-Christian notion of the Fall, others to utopian or escapist modes of thought. Encourage them to see how their general repertoires (and perhaps their literary ones) are being engaged.

"You Fit into Me" lends itself both to an exploration of metaphoric and gender-specific reading strategies. Students are intrigued by the eerie nature of the simile. Some students will also see the poem as a sardonic rejection of romantic love, the "made for each other" cliche. "The Animals in That Country" also can bring out a variety of views: some students will see the seductive appeal of art and fantasy, even while such a world isn't real.

STEPHEN DUNN, "DAY AND NIGHT HANDBALL"

Response Statement Assignment

Do you find this poem most satisfying with a literal or a metaphorical reading?

Teaching Notes

A great poem for sports fans; once the careful and loving details have been followed, the poem seems to work wonderfully on a literal reading, as being about handball (or another sport). There's a richness of detail that makes the poem very satisfying on that level. But many students, more attuned to metaphor or (a great discussion of the way individual repertoires work here) not keen on sports, will want to move the poem quickly into the metaphor.

RAYMOND CARVER, "PROSSER"

Response Statement Assignment

What attitude toward Prosser did you take? What aspects of your own general repertoire influenced your reading?

Teaching Notes

This is a moving poem that should appeal to readers' memories of their childhoods, especially if they have moved away from the home in which they grew up. The perspective of the adult looking back is, perhaps, one that becomes more powerful as you grow older. The changing perspectives of different times of life can be usefully adopted to show compatible, though distinct, readings.

PATRICK LANE, "PASSING INTO STORM"

Response Statement Assignment

How do you read the term "white man" as the poem proceeds?

Teaching Notes

Do your students want to read many or few of the details metaphorically? "White man" is arguably a key phrase in this regard: you can give the poem a powerful, bitter reading, or a mildly comical one, avoiding the intensity that the phrase can evoke.

DENNIS LEE, "THURSDAY"

Response Statement Assignment

Does this poem confirm or challenge your view of what poetry should do?

Teaching Notes

A powerful statement of poetry as the record of detail, an obsessive voice, piling up details and impressions. Some students will respond strongly, negatively or positively; some will try to imitate it; others will be appalled by the "disorder." Let such varying interpretations reveal both the reading strategies and the general (or even literary) repertoires.

ROBERT HASS, "PICKING BLACKBERRIES WITH A FRIEND WHO HAS BEEN READING JACQUES LACAN"

Response Statement Assignment

What connections do you find between the abstract and concrete levels of this poem?

Teaching Notes

The abstract and concrete interact intriguingly in Hass's poem. Explain in a little detail, perhaps, who Lacan was, and how many contemporary theories of language regard words (or other languages) as the only reality we possess, or how Lacan insisted that in the broadest sense the unconscious is structured like a language, and that things can be mediated only by language. You might compare the ending of Hass's "Meditation at Lagunitas," treated in detail in the Reading and Responding Section. Hass's poem can be read as a playful commentary on the seeming absurdity of Lacan's views. And yet, of course, Hass can make his point only in words!

WILLIAM PITT ROOT, "UNDER THE UMBRELLA OF BLOOD"

Response Statement Assignment

Do you find the connection between the last four lines and the rest of the poem convincing?

Teaching Notes

Some of our students have found this poem revolting or creepy; others, haunting and powerful (some knowing, others not, the Shelleyan notion of poetry trying to capture the glow of the coal as it fades in the darkness). The crux is whether the analogy between the execution and poetry works. Some will ignore that and rather find the scene itself, without its metaphorical extension, powerful enough. A Borges story, "The End of the Duel," which is frequently anthologized, deals with a similar situation as a tale.

PAUL SIMON, "AMERICA"

Response Statement Assignment

What aspects of American ideology does this song deal with? To what extent do you identify with them?

Teaching Notes

This is one of Paul Simon's most interesting songs on the connection of "public" world and "private" experience. It is most accessibly recorded on the live double album of the Simon and Garfunkel concert in Central Park.

Some discussion of its song-like quality is in order, but it's especially good for introducing a discussion on how popular song can incorporate, at a very obvious level, the dominant (and occasionally some of the counter-dominant) values of our society's ideology.

BOB DYLAN, "THE TIMES THEY ARE A-CHANGIN'"
"I SHALL BE RELEASED"

Response Statement Assignment

What difference is there between reading these lyrics and hearing them sung?

Teaching Notes

This assignment can clearly be adapted to any of the contemporary lyrics we've included in the <u>Lexington</u> <u>Introduction</u>. Dylan has recorded and rerecorded "The Times..." song many times, and it has been recorded by other performers, including Peter, Paul, and Mary. "I Shall Be Released" has also been widely recorded, notably by Joan Baez, as well as by Dylan himself.

Music makes a difference to the way we read song lyrics. That much is obvious, yet you can raise the question of the kinds of difference. Do the words stand by themselves? Does the music reinforce or contrast with the words? Can we speak of the <u>ideological</u> function of music? These are all interesting and arguable questions.

NIKKI GIOVANNI, "NIKKI ROSA"

Response Statement Assignment

Does the closeness of this poem to everyday speech strike you as appropriate for poetry?

Teaching Notes

A frequent barrier to students' liking contemporary poetry is the expectation that poetry is formal, usually characterized by rhyme and elevated diction. A great deal of modern poetry, however, tries to reproduce the sense of a voice in process. Students' expectations about poetry can be nicely highlighted by such a poem.

MICHAEL ONDAATJE, "KING KONG MEETS WALLACE STEVENS"

Response Statement Assignment

What effect do you feel is achieved by the juxtaposition of the two names?

Teaching Notes

A bizarre combination? Too subjective to be effective? Is the whole poem a playful but not profound joke? What about the seemingly personal intervention of line 3? What is the <u>effect</u> on a reader of reading (or hearing) the poem? Does it seem "dramatic" in any way? These are all questions that might well become quite different responses. Encourage the differences; the poem provides a good starting point.

PIER GIORGIO DI CICCO, "THE MAN CALLED BEPPINO"

Response Statement Assignment

How do you respond to Beppino? With sympathy? Horror? Indifference? Describe your feelings and account for them in terms of your own repertoire.

Teaching Notes

Many readers will probably feel compassion, but others might say that it's a tough world, and only the best or smartest survive. "This is what it is to be an immigrant," said one of our students. Like Wayman's poem on unemployment, discussed in the Poetry Introduction, this poem works well to bring out readers' different views on work, class, nationality, and identity.

BRUCE SPRINGSTEEN, "DARKNESS ON THE EDGE OF TOWN"

Response Statement Assignment

What, in your opinion, is the "darkness on the edge of town"?

Teaching Notes

Springsteen's songs tend to be so direct, often brutally and repetitively, that it is interesting to see such weight on a line in which there's a powerful metaphor. Readers will probably respond more to the conscious suggestiveness of the line, whereas listeners to the song (found on the album of the same name) may simply skip over it, absorbing it into the overall effect. What kinds of "darkness" do your students imagine? Why does the image hold such power?

LAURIE ANDERSON, "O SUPERMAN"

Response Statement Assignment

What, in your view, does "superman" stand for?

Teaching Notes

Many students will have seen Laurie Anderson in performance, or seen her movies--she has been a cult figure on the campus circuit since the early 1980s. The song "O Superman" recorded both as a single (it went Top Ten in Britain) and on the album "Big Science" makes an eerily haunting poem, especially in the way it evokes many all too familiar ideological motifs of our time--power as protection, escapism as freedom. Students will probably respond to the puns, such as "petrochemical arms," very easily, and that response can become the starting point for a discussion on the cultural origin of metaphor.

Reading and Responding to Drama

Note that unlike the other genres, all the plays are included in the Reading and Responding section; there is no separate anthology section. Here we discuss the questions to be raised in classes and the responses which come from students. We place the discussion of Stoppard's play first, since the discussion of the sample student response and further questions come before Antigone, out of chronological order.

A NOTE ON TEACHING DRAMA

In the introduction to the Drama section, we focus on the major challenge in teaching plays. Not only are they longer than stories or poems, but they may often seem disembodied on the page of a textbook. Plays, as we make clear, are meant primarily for production. Your students will probably need some guidance on issues of theatricality, stage history, and production possibilities, but in our experience, students become quickly interested in such matters, especially those with a little theater-going experience.

We suggest very strongly that if a live production of one of the plays becomes available you make use of it, encouraging or requiring your class to see it. Next best is clearly a video-taped production--the BBC Shakespeare plays, seen over the last few years on PBS, are widely available, as are a host of other productions, including the recent production of Death of a Salesman starring Dustin Hoffman, which our students liked enormously (an impression, incidentally, not unanimously shared by the editors of the Lexington Introduction, pointing perhaps to a generational difference.)

Reading aloud in class and listening to recordings can also be used, though we suggest doing so with discrete scenes. You should focus on matters of staging, perhaps using blackboard diagrams, and throughout stress the vital role of the audience.

Never forget that all your students have grown up with (perhaps "on" is the better word) television and movies, and apart from showing them how different media make different demands on a script and audience alike, you can use their media repertoires to enhance the teaching of plays.

Brief response statement assignments can be used with all the plays to prepare students for class discussion. The advantages of assigning response statements before discussing a work or an issue in class is that students will be prepared for the discussion. Useful preliminary topics when teaching drama could examine stage presentation, including such details as costume, staging, and characterizations, focusing always on one scene or part of a scene. If there are students with experience in drama, a blocking assignment (deciding where actors stand and move) could be given. Then you can focus on more technical matters such as timing, lighting, interaction, props, and so forth.

TOM STOPPARD, ROSENCRANTZ AND GUILDENSTERN ARE DEAD

Teaching Notes

Cultural and Literary Repertoire: Your students will see quickly that Stoppard relies on his audience to fill in gaps from their cultural and literary repertoires because most people have read or seen a version of Hamlet. They know, in some general sense at least, who Rosencrantz and Guildenstern are, and those who know Hamlet better can recall how they responded to these characters, and to their roles in the play.

Interpretations can vary. The most obvious is that Rosencrantz and Guildenstern represent people who bow to authority and who act without really thinking. They immediately accept the diagnosis that Hamlet is insane and thus betray a friend; but having been misguided, they really believe that Hamlet may be dangerous to the state. They are jealous of Hamlet, and don't fathom his ambiguity, disliking what they don't understand.

Such an interpretation revolves around the question of power--who initiates it, whether it exists independent of the men and women caught up in it, what it feels like to be a "minor player" in politics (or the theater). You might get the students to visualize a production of the play that had Rosencrantz and Guildenstern in modern dress, with all the other characters in "authentic" Elizabethan dress; or one with them all in modern dress.

This brings up the crucial matter of Stoppard's play as a distinctive modern reading of Shakespeare, in the sense we've spoken of readings of texts throughout the Lexington Introduction. What elements of Stoppard's reading of Hamlet come from his distinctively twentieth-century experience? The nobility of the tragic action is made farcical; the inevitability of tragic doom turns into a farcical mixture of accident and pointless necessity; the strong anger of the avenging hero is undermined by the self-serving scheming of very modern-sounding hangers-on. Do the students feel this is an attack on a view of how life was in the past? Or on a view of life that was only imagined but which never really existed? Or is it merely modern cynicism?

Here you may introduce students to the world of Ionesco whose work is also represented here, and the theater of the absurd--all influences on the literary repertoire of Rosencrantz and Guildenstern. You might talk about Alfred Jarry and the first play of the absurd, Ubu Roi. Perhaps read some sections from that play and from The Cenci of Anton Artaud and analyze his contribution to absurd theater, especially the cathartic effects of cruelty. You can also ask your students why they feel that playwrights searched for new theatrical modes as an alternative to the conventions of realism that were and still are so popular. A good topic to explore is the strengths and limitations of realism in the theater.

Consistency Building: Rosencrantz and Guildenstern Are Dead roughly follows the plot of Shakespeare's play; it has a beginning, middle, and end, as Aristotle prescribed more than two thousand years ago. But why should it be seen in those terms? Should a play follow a consistent pattern? Continually, much that occurs in life does not seem to form a consistent pattern, yet people often seem to expect consistency in the theater. What strategies, then, can the reader bring to this play? The events do not happen in any sensible order, yet often readers look for order in disorder. What readers find in that disorder—how they fill in the gaps of the play—will depend on their repertoires and on the types of strategies you encourage them to adopt while reading it. We suggest that as an alternative to consistency building, readers revel in the chance, haphazard nature of events in the play, that they open the play up and let it open them up to multiple, often contradictory, interpretive options.

SOPHOCLES, ANTIGONE

Teaching Notes

History: To fill out their general repertoires, you might tell your students something of Greek culture and tragedy: the importance of the oath in that society; the use of the chorus in the play; the unity of time, space, and place; the myth surrounding the role of Antigone; and even the relationships between the Greek concept of fate and modern psychoanalytic ideas such as the Oedipal complex, especially if they have read the Freud essay in The Lexington Introduction. You might also talk about the popularity of the Antigone story among some modern writers, including Anouilh, the modern French playwright, who has written a version of it. If they read the Anouilh, an interesting question might be whether they respond more easily to the modern version than to the older one, and why or why not.

Reader Expectations and the Sense of Duty: If your students have an initial difficulty in understanding Antigone's motivation, try to translate it into more modern terms. Look at lines such as, "And yet what greater glory could I find than giving my brother funeral?" and consider why any sister should feel that way. Some may find parallels with people who have not been able to locate the bodies of dead sons or husbands who fought in Vietnam. If certainty about her brother's death is not Antigone's motivation, then what is it—in terms that modern readers can understand? Raising such issues can make students aware of how different historical repertoires may affect their readings of the play.

Another question related to history focuses on why Antigone's brothers were fighting each other. Some students, those who look at the situation in a very literal sense, might consider that Antigone's rebellious brother was too ambitious, too caught up in his own ego struggles and therefore deserving of what happened to him. Others may disagree and feel that Antigone did what they might have done to uphold the honor of the family. A more accessible means of approach is through the question of power. That's probably the way the play can best be seen today, since power (as Michel Foucault once remarked) seems to be "in the air" nowadays! Focus on the political implications of the play: perhaps Antigone's rebellious brother wanted power rather than a better state; maybe the situation under Creon,was a stable, good, peaceful one, and to disrupt the system seemed foolish. Where does one's duty really belong, to society, or one's family? Does Antigone care far too much about an honor that might have been unimportant when compared with the welfare of people in general? Perhaps she can be read as dominated by pride, in which case the play might be regarded as a psychological study of an ego that carried her to extreme measures in order to satisfy it. But (as with the other questions raised) never forget to consider such matters in the context of staging. How would these readings work in performance?

Creon and the Divided Self: Creon can be interpreted as more reasonable, less emotional, and more concerned with the good of the country. Perhaps an interesting interpretation that might arise is whether he is a divided character, one who has mixed motives. He can be regarded as concerned about Antigone as a personal threat to him, and about her as a political threat to the peace of the country. Does Creon feel personally defensive about the power he possesses, or does he feel an obligation to the responsibility he holds? In a way, perhaps Creon is sincere when he blames Antigone and her family for destroying his personal peace, yet his desire for power may be a more central matter. Would a modern production provide a more liberal, humane interpretation of Creon, perhaps depicting him as being honestly afraid of more violence? Or would it depict Creon as a cruel and ruthless lover of power? An interesting study of division would result--that of a man who wanted all things: the loyalty of Antigone, the peace of his country, and the power of being the ruler.

Feminist Reading: We ask our students whether or not they benefit from trying a feminist reading of the play. Do they think it is appropriate to read an older text from a distinctively contemporary perspective? Perhaps such an ancient play might deal with male/female issues in ways unfamiliar to us. You might raise the question of how women and men are presented in the Greek myths, exploring the events in the myths where women are raped, and the attributes of the male gods as contrasted with those of the goddesses. That Antigone plays the role of upholding the honor of family might seem pre-feminist to some, while her willingness to defy male authority in fighting for her beliefs will seem feminist to others. Can the ability to fight, commonly associated with men, be feminist? Could upholding one's values seem feminist? Some students may feel that Creon is not presented in the "macho" way they expect in Greek myths; he is not a conventional hero but rather a political leader who assumes power and tries to keep the peace. Again, raise the question of how these different readings might affect the staging of the play. Always keep in mind the question of audience reaction and the challenge of mounting a production of an ancient play.

SHAKESPEARE, HAMLET

Teaching Notes

Hamlet is, if not Shakespeare's greatest play, certainly his most intriguing, at least in terms of the approach to literature taken in the Lexington Introduction. Its critical history is one of multiple, creative readings, what Harold Bloom would term misreadings. It illustrates better than any other play by Shakespeare the lack of any "original" or "authentic" text. When Shakespeare's friends assembled the First Folio of his plays in 1621, they had a number of quite different earlier editions from which to choose--adaptations, rewritings, alternative versions. In short, the history of the text itself supports the approach we advocate.

We suggest that you don't overwhelm students with historical "background," although it is interesting that in 1600, when the play was probably written, the question of succession to the English throne was a stormy one: Queen Elizabeth was in her sixties, childless, and a number of would-be successors had already advanced their claims. The historical parallels are <u>not</u> exact, but the issue was a current one.

<u>Multiple Meanings</u>: <u>Hamlet</u> offers students the opportunity to locate their own readings among the many critical interpretations of the play by directors and critics. They may well be surprised at the number and variety of these interpretations. You can get them not merely to decide whether they agree or disagree with Coleridge, or Bradley, or Jones, or Knights (or you!) but to examine how those critical interpretations reflect some of the wider social attitudes of the times and the cultures within which they were written. The same goes for the stage history. Likewise, you want students to see if they can understand, after reading the play, why the play appeals so greatly both to the public and to the critics, and in this connection to see how crucial the play's ambiguities are to the creative imaginations of the public and the critics--as well as to directors, producers, and actors.

The Drama introduction contains a fair bit of material on <u>Hamlet</u>, but you might also ask students to do some library research on critical interpretations and reviews of various productions that they find interesting. These classes can be fun as students exchange information and comment on what they find in a variety of sources: old reviews in the <u>New York Times</u>, in nineteenth-century periodicals, in scholarly journals, in the <u>New Yorker</u>, and others. You can then return to the general question of how they can reconcile these changes with the notion that a classic text is thought to be "timeless."

What does "timeless" or "universal" mean? What is a "classic"? If <u>Hamlet</u> is indeed a classic, what boundary conditions are there of interpretation? Perhaps try to work round to the idea that maybe a classic is such precisely because it <u>doesn't</u> have a fixed meaning, and that it seems continually to open up new and provocative readings. Then focus on <u>Hamlet</u> itself. Has any of the students' critical reading altered their original positions? What wider cultural interests do they have that help produce their readings? After all, if we can show why Coleridge or Jones came up with certain readings, then equivalent factors must be operating on the students themselves.

You can, on a more elementary level, obtain much the same result from getting students to summarize in a hundred words or so what the play is about. You will doubtlessly get responses that stress the psychological, the political, ·the erotic, or the familial dimensions of the play, and many more. If students focus on Hamlet himself (a common preoccupation since the Romantics, of course), a spectrum of Hamlets will undoubtedly emerge: the troubled philosophy student, the cunning avenger, the play enthusiast, the indecisive weakling, the self-obsessed (or mother-obsessed, or father-obsessed!) adolescent. And more! Once again, probe for some account of what in the text's repertoire and what in reader's help produce such readings.

Staging: We suggest that you keep reminding your students that Hamlet is a play, not a psychological case-history, or a novel. It is a script waiting to be enacted, whether on stage, in a classroom, or just in a student's mind. You might want to use Hamlet to illustrate something of the Elizabethan stage-- remember, not to provide information about the or an "authentic" production but to show the possibilties for the play within one particular theatrical milieu. Talk about how the Elizabethan "thrust" stage had its audience on three sides (as well as "behind" stage and, at times, on the stage), which fostered intimacy between players and audience, especially during the soliloquies. Many of the details of the play, too, might have been written by Shakespeare to fit the possibilities and limits of his acting company. For instance, prepubescent boys played women's roles (a practice referred to in Hamlet) and women were forbidden by law to act. Modern acting companies are obviously very different--in fact in many acting companies and college theater departments, it is usually much easier to get women actors than men.

The discussion can then be broadened to an analysis of other stage and acting situations--the rise of the proscenium stage, the emergence of the "star" system, the nineteenth century's preference for illusionist spectacle, the special demands of film, and so forth. When you discuss the students' own conceptions of the play, always ask how will it play (and not just in Peoria!).

Psychological Repertoire: Our society still places an enormous emphasis on individuality--see Raymond Williams's essay from Keywords (in the Essay section) for some explanation of this phenomenon. It's seen, of course, at its most apparent, in the reification of the star system in Hollywood movies, and spills over into theatrical productions. Of course, it permeates much of the residual thinking of our whole culture.

Hamlet is therefore a perfect text for the post-Cartesian to discuss! It epitomizes the post-Renaissance Western society's reification of the individual, and criticism and production bear this out, whatever their other differences. Yet, paradoxically, as we all become aware of the subjected nature of individuality, we can see how Hamlet, the character, is not only the major focus of individuality in the play, but the major example of what it is to be a subject.

You will probably discover that students (like Coleridge) find it easy to "identify" with Hamlet, and likewise easily depict him in their own, or their society's image.

We find that Hamlet allows students to discuss, with a great deal of understanding, how their psychological repertoires influence their interpretations of and interests in specific scenes and pieces of dialogue. Interesting discussion follows questions like these: when Hamlet discusses his sanity/insanity, how does your own definition of those terms influence your attitudes toward his mental state? When Hamlet jokes ominously with Polonius, how do you respond to his use of double meanings? How do you feel about the way in which Hamlet treats Ophelia, someone he seems to have loved? Do you believe Hamlet when he says that he will not kill the King at prayers because the latter will then go to heaven? How do you feel about the relationship between Hamlet and Gertrude, especially in their conversation before the death of Polonius? Do you find Hamlet a psychologically healthy person when you read about his friendship with Horatio, or his friendship with Laertes and his attempts not to kill him?

Of course, all such questions are at a fairly elementary level, but they become more complex when you push them back to their cultural origins and look at their implications. Why does it seem "natural" to focus on Hamlet's character? Or even on other characters? What if we constructed a reading of the play that sees it less as a tragedy of the individual (though a tragedy of <u>excessive</u> individuality might be interesting) and more as a tragedy of a community? Or a tragedy of inadequate dealing with political issues? Berthold Brecht wrote an additional scene for his actors, in which the dispute between Denmark and Norway was resolved by negotiation, not war, and the play ended without some of the bloodshed. Verbal negotiation is the "modern way," say some lines in the scene. Raymond Williams has also argued in <u>Modern Tragedy</u> that tragedy as traditionally conceived is the product of a society that sees conflicts as unavoidable, the universe as deterministic and ruled by unseen, doom-like powers. These residual beliefs are still strong in our society and, as some of your students may perceive, continue to distort our lives today. This kind of analysis will have some relevance when you discuss <u>Death of a Salesman</u>.

<u>History</u>: The question of the culture-specific nature of tragedy brings up the issue of historical difference. While <u>Hamlet</u> seems to be a play that speaks to all people in all times, it was written at a specific time and has characteristics typical of that time. We ask students to look again at the scenes involving the Ghost in order to show them a section that probably must be reinterpreted by modern readers. Students say that the words of the guards, of Horatio's conversation with them, and of Horatio's warnings to Hamlet, seem to indicate that the characters in the play believe in ghosts. Most students will assume that the ghost would have seemed real to much of the Elizabethan audience. How would the ghost be played today for audiences who obviously don't believe in ghosts? Thus we lead our students into a discussion of how difficult it is for them to stay within the bounds of a traditional reading of the play, something that a spectator in Shakespeare's time probably could have done with more ease. The movement from "supernatural" to "psychological" to "political" interpretations of the play reflects wider cultural changes than just theatrical or critical fashions.

HENRIK IBSEN, <u>THE</u> <u>WILD</u> <u>DUCK</u>

Teaching Notes

<u>Gaps</u>: Since readers necessarily must fill the gaps between what the characters in a play say and what readers think the characters mean, Ibsen's play offers a good opportunity for students to see this process. Clearly Ibsen provides more

information in stage directions and in character descriptions than does Shakespeare. Behind the play lie many of the assumptions of the novel and "realism." Nonetheless the reader must still fill in gaps about what Hedvig feels as she pulls the trigger of the gun, about how other characters, especially Hedvig's mother, will deal with her death. Ibsen may give much information before the play begins, but what the characters feel must still be filled out. A director or set designer, too, must make significant decisions.

<u>Cultural Repertoire and Multiple Interpretations</u>: We ask our students whether their interpretations tend to change as they progress in reading the play. Here we get a variety of responses about the relationship between their own repertoires and their ability to deal simultaneously with multiple interpretations. Some have ambivalent feelings about the life of the family: while initially thinking these people are normal, they come to find them to be neurotic and self-serving. At first many students like Gina, thinking that she's a good mother, but they then may alter that feeling because of her sacrifices to practicality and her inability to understand Hedvig. They might feel somewhat sorry for Old Ekdal, yet get angry at his allowing Hedvig, at her age, to feel as she does about the significance of the wild duck. They might feel anger towards Hjalmar Ekdal because of his selfishness and innocence, yet be understanding of his ego problems. They probably have mixed feelings about Gregers, who makes a great mistake, yet does so for what he thinks are the best of reasons. This kind of "identification" seems natural, especially if students visualize the play realistically. Our students also find themselves confused about the family's relationships; they find that love among members of the family does exist but the love seems precarious, selfish, and without understanding of individual needs, especially Hedvig's. Many of our students recognized that their interpretations of characters and events in the play depended heavily on what they brought to it from their own cultural attitudes about family life. Again, once you get a variety of responses from your students, ask them how they might want to stage productions that would emphasize their particular interpretations.

<u>Metaphor--Reality and Illusion</u>: You might want to call into question the necessity of a transparently "realistic" reading. Is the play "realistic" because the direction of the action moves in a chronological way, and because dialogue, characters, and events seem to parallel those of daily life? Students will probably perceive a real, though unseen, wild duck, a believable invalid child who is going blind, a family with perhaps a few more problems than most, a home with friends and others, a normal dinner party at the Werles, a mixture of generations within the family, and a familiar reality in the setting and character descriptions.

The symbolism of the play, however, calls into question this realistic reading. After all, people in real life are generally not analyzed symbolically! Since the symbolism is fairly obvious and (some readers think) a bit heavy, you can quite easily demonstrate to students the contradictory ways in which they are reading the play, not to show that they are "wrong," but to illustrate the conventional nature of realism in a play. It is only because the convention is familiar to students from television and film that they are able to regard it as "natural."

What do students think about the strong, unexpected identification of Hedvig with the wild duck? Ask for ideas about what the wild duck needs. Answers will vary: freedom to be in its natural environment rather than in an attic; freedom to be able to fly; freedom from needing care of strange beings among whom it cannot feel comfortable. You might then ask about the need for love and Hedvig's final sacrifice to show her love. Is it Gregers who pushes her to that sacrifice, misguided because he means she should kill the duck? The questions you would then grapple with are: Why does the misunderstanding occur? Why is Gregers confused about reality and illusion? Why does Gina possess a strong sense of her own reality? Why is Edkal unable to face reality and why does he respond as he does when he learns about Gina's past? Why does Hedvig respond tragically to the illusions around her?

PIRANDELLO, SIX CHARACTERS IN SEARCH OF AN AUTHOR

Teaching Notes

Literary Repertoire and Absurd Theater: If your students have read other "absurdist" texts they will have less difficulty in reading this play. If they come to it before reading other such works, we may direct them, as we do in the response statement questions in the introduction, to specific parts of this play when the actors actually discuss the absurd. In Six Characters, the central "absurdity" exists in having characters search for an author. That can be a clue that unusual reading strategies are needed. Similarly, students will realize that that they need different strategies for reading Rosencrantz and Guildenstern Are Dead from those they used for Hamlet. Try to get them to develop alternatives to making conventional assumptions about time, place, space, order of events, and consistency of the characters as real people.

Layering: In reading this play students can develop a great deal of interest in the various levels of reality and illusion. Ask them to scan the play again after they have read it in order to determine the pattern of action. Generally they can do that without too much difficulty, and they begin to recognize that in many ways life is much more confusing than the play. But they then must grapple with the question of whether they feel that the unconventional text strategies underlying the play are effective--especially if they can imagine the play being staged. Here they must consider the layering of the action, the repetition, the characters moving from roles as actors to those of real persons. Focus on those parts of the play when a character does not want to play a character, when the real actor gets confused by the "character in search of," when the child does not want to watch a scene, all moving to the final tragedy of the play. Does that tragedy stem from the inability of the actors, real or not, who are searching for an author, to find their own reality? What does their need for an author represent?

Answers may well vary from the idea that the characters are really insane people in need of a psychiatrist, to that they are looking for God in the form of an author who can provide meaning for their lives and explain what happens to them. Still others, who are more philosophically inclined, will want to explore the characters' ontological status as the ideas of an author and see them as raising problems about interpreting any characters in a dramatic text.

Pirandello layers one illusion/reality on top on another perhaps in order to parallel the seemingly absurd relationships among events, characters, and the whole pattern of life. If events occur haphazardly, if actors move as though moved by some unseen force, and thus need an author to get them straightened out, then there's the possibilty of an allegorical reading or at least the sense that the play is "relevant" to life outside the boundaries of the play. So students might discuss such issues as: the Oedipal conflicts between father and daughter; the "mousy" quality of the mother; the pull between duty and desire of the father; the psychological pressure on the young boy; the occurrence of events over which the characters have no control; the conflicts inherent in middle-class morality--all of which can be extended to a view of the world in general.

EUGENE IONESCO, THE GAP

Teaching Notes

Consistency Building/Naturalizing the Text: Try to get your students to understand that as readers of the play, they are faced with what can be seen as total inconsistency. Most will, no doubt, try to straighten it out! They may want to work first with what is realistic in the play: the language, the wife, the friend, the academician, and the facts that a house exists, that an exam has been given, and that the academician has failed the exam. What then stands between this reality and the overall effect of the play? Why would an academician take an exam? Some of your students may say that perhaps this situation attempts to satirize the tenure system! Or is it just that Ionesco is laughing at what the world takes seriously--honors, degrees, exams, rationality? So the play can become simply funny, rather like Monty Python or the Marx Brothers. Students may choose to analyze the responses of the friend, the academician talking like a baby and tearing off his medals, the others not wanting to "play" with the academician because he failed, the police, the spotlights on the list of those who failed. Get them to speculate on the theatricality of such incidents as they do about Saturday Night Live. How would they perform them? What effects would they want to get?

Ideology: Ask what beliefs and attitudes readers may bring to the play. What beliefs and attitudes might the play evoke? Talk about attitudes toward the university, or the college, the respect paid to it, the high tuition, the university as a place to get degrees which stand for a great deal in our society. What do such values imply? Students might say that they imply that more education is better, but that perhaps the author of this play feels otherwise. If you want to continue such a track (it becomes a self-parody after a while to contemplate it, given the humor of the play, but you might well find students think the play should be taken "seriously"), then point out that professors often lose their jobs because they haven't published enough, probably quite similar to the situation mentioned in The Gap.

But it really seems very self-defeating to encourage such readings, except to get some discussion going about why anyone would want to read the play in such a fashion. Is it because they are "literalists"? Or because they have in their repertoires the residual puritan distrust of fun? Or because they've been trained to find serious "themes" everywhere? You might discover in some readers the same lack of strategies to deal with the humor of e.e. cummings, Ronald Sukenick, or Donald Barthelme. Try to get around such approaches by focusing on the performance aspect of the play. It's a good one to act out in class: solemn "thematic" readings tend to emerge from not visualizing it as a play!

ARTHUR MILLER, DEATH OF A SALESMAN

Teaching Notes

Ideology and Literary Repertoire: Many of your students will have read The Great Gatsby in high school or other works dealing with such aspects of American ideology as the widespread American desire for success, and the great importance of money and fame. Your students may well perceive that many writers criticize those kinds of values, yet they nonetheless find themselves in college concerned about what their careers will be and how much money they will earn. Selling on the road the way Willy Loman did may be outmoded, but what about the engineers who spend their time on planes and in hotels because they need to market their company's products? Death of a Salesman certainly reflects on as well as depicts the ideology of "the way to get ahead."

Students will certainly have in their general repertoires a great deal that will confirm such an ideology, and you might use parallels between Willy Loman's dreams and hopes and the idealization of the rich in Dynasty or Lifestyles of the Rich and Famous. Students (like the rest of us) are sites of contradiction, at once able to be critical of the destructiveness of such myths and yet enjoying them. There will no doubt be general agreement about the attraction of American consumerism ("people love to walk in shopping malls for recreation," as one of our students rather arbitrarily noted!) and also its antithesis, an idealism that says it is wrong to worship goods/money/power. Where students will probably disagree will be in their interpretation of Willy: is he a fool to be taken in, a victim of the American ideology, a man too small to be the success he wanted to be, a bad parent because he looked to his children to satisfy his ideals, a "big" man who knew how to be unselfish when he realized he had failed; a coward who couldn't face reality? That's where you may get some very interesting matchings or clashings of repertoires.

Gaps and the Tragic Hero: If you talk with students about the nature of tragedy, give some historical perspective on the diverse ways in which tragedy has been viewed, and how these views reflect wider changes in society. Hamlet was, of course, a prince, and the heroes/heroines from most of the older plays they have read are generally also from the upper classes. Only by the later nineteenth century did the the tragic figure appear as a "little" man, perhaps a person important only to his family. An audience two hundred years ago could probably never have identified itself with a figure like Willy, even though many of them (but probably not today's students) may have known Elizabethan middle-class tragedies like A Woman Killed with Kindness. One very interesting topic for discussion might well be why the lower classes in traditional plays seem to be identified with comic effects.

Clearly, Willy is not a "tragic hero" in the older sense. One line of argument is that, of course, he is a tragic figure for a more democratic time, someone we "identify" with rather than look up to. Students may feel that they could understand Willy's failures because of their own family lives: his failure as a parent, failure as a provider, failure to inspire respect, failure to survive. Some students may argue that they could bring a strong feminist reading to the play, that expectations for Willy's success were "male" expectations in our family structure and in our society, even in the face of changing roles. In this way many may feel, especially as they reread the requiem in class, that Willy assumes the stature of a tragic figure. Still others might think that a living Willy might be even more tragic than a dead one; many may suggest that their own fathers could not live with Willy's failures.

Layering: We find that Death of a Salesman benefits from a discussion of the layering that comes from various interpretations and productions of the play, which has not only retained its popularity in the past forty years, but has had some interesting new productions. Discuss early productions with students; you might even find old reviews of the Lee J. Cobb version. There they read about Willy as fat and blustering, someone who eats too much and talks loudly. Then you might show them the Frederic March film, readily available, in which Willy is slower, less volatile. Most recently there's the Dustin Hoffman television production which, from our experience, students find conforms to their idea of what Willy should be: small, thin, aging, nervous, sad-looking, talking big, a psychological rather than a social tragic hero. You might focus on the effect of having a "star" like Hoffman play Willy. Does it make him seem more sympathetic? You might also get hold of the program in the PBS series American Masters, about how the Hoffman version was filmed, with Hoffman talking about his sense of the part, his identification with Willy, who was like his father, and most important, his discussions with Arthur Miller about how certain scenes should be played. This program features a number of conversations between playwright and actor, then the particular scene under discussion, and then sometimes a reworking of the scene until it suits actor, director, and playwright. Students should not feel that what is created is then the authentic reading, but one that suited particular people in a particular historical and cultural situation. Seeing or reading about diverse productions of the play can help students keep in mind that the creation of a play is a multifaceted (overdetermined) and ever-changing matter.

EDWARD ALBEE, THE SANDBOX

Teaching Notes

American Culture and the Absurd: When Albee's play first appeared it seemed that non-traditional theatre had at last reached America. Why does the boy do calisthenics throughout most of the play? Your students may well enter into the spirit of the play and respond with a variety of reasons: he has nothing else to do; he's a satire on the American emphasis on physical fitness; he is all body and no mind; he cannot face the emotional trauma of his grandmother's dying. Their responses lead them to interpreting the play as a bitter satire, a cruel look at how families can treat their aged relatives, yet again like some of the skits on Saturday Night Live. Students may comment on Mommy's euphemisms such as, "it means the time has come for poor Grandma...and I can't bear it..." and laugh at the absurdity of the boy's continuing to do calisthenics as a piece of theatrical fun. Or they may take a "heavy" view of it, that he can't tolerate his mother! Along these "thematic" lines, students may feel that the characters Mommy, Boy, and Grandma, who have no other names, suggest people who have been deprived of real feelings. On one level these people profess to love, but on another, they cannot love. While many of our students feel that such an absurd approach to American culture is exaggerated, some may want to see it as profoundly serious and focus on the poignancy of problems of the aged, such as their own grandmothers and grandfathers. The loneliness, the constraints of a "sandbox," the insincerity of Mommy's grief—all suggest our failures in dealing with generational problems in the family and problems of the aged in society. When we ask students to check autobiographical materials about Albee about his adoption, uneasy relationship with his mother, and his closeness to his grandmother, some feel that the problems in the play are in fact as much personal as social. "But what about the play in the theater?" you should continually ask!

Metaphor and Reading Strategies: If you ask students if they can treat this play as realistic in any way, you will no doubt discover that their strategies for reading realistically are better developed yet not particularly useful! Some will insist that the play is realistic because the subject matter is close to them: most are familiar with the problems of dealing in humane and loving ways with an aged grandparent, and of coping with anger at parents (who themselves may have ambivalent feelings about their parents). Others insist that they can only read the play as a metaphor that characterizes the selfishness and mechanistic qualities of our society. One of our students commented that the whole experience of the play read like a metaphor for death rather than for life.

As with many post-realist plays, we suggest you anticipate such readings, which is why we've spent a little time on them. Students (like many older people whose repertoires don't include a great deal of post-modernist literature, film, music, or theater) don't visually have a large repertoire of strategies to employ on such texts. That is why we emphasize strongly in our own classes that dramatic texts should be seen live, and that students should become aware of theater groups, serious film theaters, art galleries, and so gradually become familiar with the dynamics of contemporary culture. Many of them have suffered in high school by being kept ignorant of what was going on in poetry, drama, fiction since the 1950s or 60s (and that is longer than most of their lifetimes). This seems an appropriate point for us to urge upon teachers something most will no doubt agree with--that students need both exposure to a great variety of cultural experiences and, just as important, a vocabulary and a set of concepts by which they can describe and "read" their experiences.

It is also an appropriate place, perhaps, to emphasize just how extensive are the repertoires of most of our students in such things as television and rock music (film is another matter; most students' experiences consist largely of Hollywood products). In our courses, including our freshman literature course, we take this repertoire very seriously, and we advocate one or more courses in "Reading Twentieth-Century Culture" (the title of one of our own required courses for the English major) and incorporate aspects of it in our freshman course. You can see more material on this aspect of our work in Reading Texts, Chapter 8.

LORRAINE HANSBERRY, A RAISIN IN THE SUN

Teaching Notes

Psychological Repertoire: This is usually presented as a "social issues" play and therefore may be more reassuring to many students. You may find that your students become deeply involved in the question of whether or not Ruth should have the abortion. They may talk about the family dynamics, about the psychological pain involved in her having the abortion. But they may also discuss the psychological damage that might occur if she had the child--to her feelings of self-esteem, her inability to get an education and a better job, to live the rest of her life at poverty level. Asking students what advice they would give Ruth if they were social workers involved in this situation reveals that they base their decisions on their own attitudes toward abortion. Thus they will see, in the strongest way possible, how much their general repertoires influence the strategies they use in reading and interpreting a text.

Cultural Situatedness: Perhaps ask students to examine the differences between their own family structures and that of this family. How, you might ask, do they perceive Walter as a husband, Mama as a mother, mother-in-law, and grandmother, and the sister as an independent person bent on succeeding. Students take special interest in the sister's desire to return to her ethnic roots as well as to use Western education to create her sense of identity. Why do Ruth and Mama feel so much differently about life from Walter's sister? What has she learned? What do they know that she doesn't? And, most important, ask your students to focus on how their "cultural situatedness" influences the way in which they read this play--the strategies they bring to that reading: what they want the characters to do as opposed to what they do; how they want the characters to think; what they want for the young boy if Ruth decides to have the abortion; what they wish Walter would learn about his role in life; what they want Mama to do with the house. As one of our students put it, "The playwright frustrates me because she puts these people in situations in which the solutions are obvious to me but not to them." Other students responded that perhaps the student who made that comment is like Willy Loman, a victim of American ideology. Must everyone be ambitious in the same ways? Perhaps people can never be happy if they are caught in such conflicts in the culture they have absorbed.

Feminist and Political Reading: Some of your students--the women especially--may see Ruth and Mama as exploited by their own men and by society; others may (as it were) want to get into the play and talk to Ruth, and make her see that she must live her own life, give up Walter. Others may be most upset by white resistance to their moving into the new house and neighborhood, wanting to change that kind of thinking and behavior of the whites. Still others will identify most with Walter's sister and her hope for a new generation of emancipated blacks; while some see parallels between the roles of blacks and of women in American society. In all cases make sure that you focus on the interactions going on between the repertoires of the text and the readers, and on ways in which the students would want to see the characters depicted on stage.

Reading and Responding to Essays

We suggest that students try to examine the familiar but arbitrary distinctions between fact and fiction when reading the essays. We tell them something about what is called the "new non-fiction," novels like The Book of Daniel or reportage like In Cold Blood. We may ask why people want to read biographies of famous (and infamous people). Most important, we try to make them see that the reading strategies they bring to fiction, poetry, and drama will work for them in reading essays.

Here we have provided teaching notes for the questions used in the Reading and Responding section. We also provide response statement assignments and teaching notes for all the other essays.

HILARY MASTERS, "SO LONG, NATTY BUMPPO"

Teaching Notes

Political Reading: We find this essay to be particularly useful in helping students perceive how their political ideas influence the reading of a text when the political views of the author are apparent. Students who approved of or liked Ronald Reagan found that Masters' attitude bothered them to the extent that they felt they personally were being challenged. Such reactions can be used immediately to focus on how general and (in this case not just narrowly political) repertoires affect the reading of a text. What is important is not whether their (or Masters'.) views are correct or incorrect, but whether they see the interactive nature of the readings produced and the implications of them for further thought and action.

Literary Repertoire: This essay also provides a good example of how readers' literary repertoires influence their reactions to an essay. It is a good essay to show how a rich set of references from art, literature, and history can be used to strengthen a position. This essay is a model for a discursive argument. Even the students who don't agree with Masters see the influence of a literary repertoire in how they respond to the position of the essay, not necessarily by agreeing with its thesis, but at least with an ability to follow its argument.

FREDERICK DOUGLASS, "THE LIFE OF FREDERICK DOUGLASS" (selection)

Teaching Notes

Ideology and Prose Style: You can use this essay to illustrate for students the power of narrative, whether in fiction or in the essay or, in this case, a selection from an autobiography. They respond to the account largely because it is easy to follow and reads like a story. They may even volunteer to read the rest of the autobiography because they want to see what happened to Douglass. Most of the students will find the style to be accessible because of the narrative, and persuasive because of their own attitudes about the evils of slavery. Try to get students to see that while is Douglass is attacking the evils of slavery, he is nonetheless very much influenced by "the American Dream" of success. In short, there are ideological contradictions you can bring out here--an interesting way to introduce strong and symptomatic reading.

Literary Repertoire and History: Uncle Tom's Cabin, which many have read, can be used to make comparisons with the Douglass selection. If they have read the fiction of Ellison, Petry, Morrison or Walker, they can talk about which of these most influenced their attitudes about racial issues. You might also ask students which political or religious figures, which television shows, films, and actors, most influence contemporary American racial attitudes. Do they feel that their experiences in school--in what they have read, been taught, seen in the attitudes of administrators--have helped to increase or decrease racial tensions? What do they bring to this essay, from both their literary repertoires and background? How does this essay reinforce what they know or believe? Does the fact that it was written so long ago affect their responses? Many students will say that because Douglass deals with specific incidents, and describes them so graphically, they do not find the essay dated, and that this personal detail conveys a sense of slavery not found in. their history textbooks.

TOM WOLFE, "THE PUMP HOUSE GANG"

Teaching Notes

Prose Style: As with fiction, writers of essays or non-fiction may attempt to match the style of the prose to the content of the essay. Some students may ask, "Does Wolfe actually talk like the narrator of this essay?" Explain that writers of non-fiction, like writers of fiction, can create a narrator in order to add to the force of the argument. Before addressing what that argument might be, you might therefore ask students what they bring to the essay that influences their responses. Clearly, stories of one sort or another evoke interest. Ask students if they have ever experienced a dull talk which became interesting when the speaker stopped lecturing, and launched into a story.

Ethnographic and Ideological Reading: Students will usually feel that the scene of the essay was distinctively American, specifically Southern Californian in the beach setting, the surf board businesses and their customers, the informal clothing, and the notion of the attractiveness of anti-social attitudes. Some students will find Wolfe's treatment dated, but others will probably point out what they see as the satirical treatment of the scene: the lack of serious comments made by anyone; the display of mock courage; the imitative styles of dress; and the superficial value system, especially in attitudes toward age. They may also question Wolfe's portrayal of the New York City businessmen who market the fashions of gangs and who contrast strongly with the other characters in the essay. Today more students may react against Wolfe's negative treatment of the capitalistic system. Some may respond with a degree of anger to the way in which Wolfe satirizes the American ideology of achievement, while other students may agree with his view. Examine, therefore, the tension between consumer and ethical values. Many students may feel that Wolfe's essay focuses exclusively on the unfortunate parts of the American ideology--the greed, the laziness, the poverty, the hollow role models. "He satirizes those," said one student, "but I wonder what he does believe in." You may find that to be a common reaction. We have our students discuss the ways in which they use their own repertoires to infer what Wolfe may himself value.

ADRIENNE E. HARRIS, "WOMEN, BASEBALL, AND WORDS"

Teaching Notes

Language and a Feminist Reading: This essay can be used to discuss the relationships between language and culture, especially how gender differences in language are culturally produced. You might usefully focus on the general issues raised by asking students if they feel that there are "naturally" different male/female languages. While some will say that we all speak English, and that words don't carry gendered connotations, others will feel that there are words used by only one gender. Some students will bring up examples of words that were more typical of male usage than of female usage. That's an approach to encourage--to show that gender is socially constructed, not "natural," and that while patriarchal society is slowly being changed, the acculturation is very deep. Many of your students will believe there are some words that are considered to be ladylike, masculine, dirty, or sexist. Put the word female on the board as an example and ask for all of the words that can mean female, such as lady, chick, kid, baby, wench, and discuss their connotative meanings. You might then discuss male/female body language and explore whether certain body movements are more "appropriate" to women than men and vice versa. The question to focus on is: Where do these values come from?

Harris's essay can provoke strong arguments in class discussion about whether or not baseball, because it has a male language, excludes women. No doubt you will get a variety of responses. Some will feel Harris is all wrong. Others will claim the real problem with the relationship between women and baseball is that they don't play it professionally the way women play tennis, and that women are only "subjective actors" because they don't play the game. While some will agree that baseball can exclude women, and that Harris is right because "locker room talk" stops when women invade a male space, there may be students who will mention that their mother or sister or girlfriend loves baseball and goes to all the games without their father and brothers. What kind of process of acculturation is going on here? How do these women feel in relation to the men? Do they feel odd that they are watching a sport played only by men?

Ideology and Baseball: Such issues lead to wider ones. Many students find Harris's arguments about the general ideology of sports, the positioning of the body, the working against the clock, the role of organized sports in class struggle to be interesting, and they often will animatedly discuss her ideas. The essay provides an intriguing example of the way ideology permeates even the most beloved and perhaps seemingly "innocent" leisure activities. We try to apply Harris's arguments to a number of different sports. Football lends itself especially well to such a discussion. The mythology of the game--the costumes, the mixture of military and ballet-like moves, the focus on the star quality of certain players like the quarterback, the class, military or individualistic character of team s' names, the intermingling with the economic entrepreneurialism of capitalism--makes football an extremely visible subject for ideological analysis. The Super Bowl is an especially good topic to extend Harris's argument. Get your students to write on such topics as "The Ideology of the Super Bowl," or articulate which dominant American values come out in the game. Like baseball, football provides a fascinating and relatively painless focus for ideological analysis.

Anthology of Essays

MICHEL–GUILLAUME–JEAN DE CREVECOEUR, "WHAT IS AN AMERICAN?"

Response Statement Assignment

1. How do you respond to Crevecoeur's sense of what America means to him? What do you feel he wants you to understand, believe, and accept? Is he persuasive? Do you find some of his views dated or do they seem pertinent to your views of America today? How does your repertoire contribute to your response to the ideology of his argument?

2. Many people see Crevecoeur as naive, perhaps too optimistic. How do you respond to that opinion? Would you use much of the information or some of the arguments in this essay if you were debating the questions of what America really is, what it ought to be, and how people perceive it?

Teaching Notes

Social Repertoire and History: Call your students' attention to the essay's form of argument, the way in which the author builds his case about America. Crevecoeur does admit to certain problems in America, even though he sees it as a wonderful country. Focus on the contradictions in his view. Many students will note his comments on the lack of law and order on the frontier and its consequent moral problems, and see this criticism as still in some ways relevant to problems of social order today. Questions that will arise might include: How much money does one put into a police force? The armed forces? Protecting victims? Punishing law breakers? Reforming prisons?

Focus on how these issues grow out of recurring questions and contradictions within the ideology of America. Students may point to other of Crevecoeur's arguments about the virtues of America which they find particularly persuasive: the way in which children help in this new country, the difference between Europe and America with regard to class structure, the mingling of ethnic groups in America. These examples suggest the importance of individual opportunity and freedom in America.

Ideology and Argument: Students differ in their responses to Crevecoeur. Some find the essay too optimistic in its views of human nature, while others see it as having contemporary relevance through its expression of "traditional American ideals." Some will argue that this kind of self–congratulation can be harmful, allowing people to forget the hunger, poverty, and other problems in America. Some may acknowledge that patriotism includes being critical of one's ideology and of how that ideology is enacted in reality. But others may feel that too much emphasis can be placed on the criticism and not enough on the rewards of living in America. We sometimes ask students to use this essay as a model for a debate on the differences between their ideologies and their expectations about America in which they substitute more current issues.

SIGMUND FREUD, "THE DREAM AS WISH-FULFILMENT"

Response Statement Assignments

1. How do you respond to Freud's theory of wish-fulfilment as the basis for dreams? Can you recognize such elements in your current dreams? What about the dreams that others tell you about? What about the dreams you have encountered in your literary repertoire? Your family life? Your changing dreams as you have grown up?

2. How do you feel about Freud's idea that dreams are capable of teaching us a great deal about ourselves? How does your background influence you to accept or reject this idea? Is this idea a new one or an old one? What is its relation to popular notions about dreams derived from the Bible, for example? In what way does this notion deal with metaphors?

Teaching Notes

Psychological Repertoire: Some might find this essay too technical, especially if they only have superficial knowledge of Freud, like the popular notions of Freudian slips of the tongue, the Oedipal complex, and the "unconscious." These students tend to place "The Dream as Wish-Fulfilment" into the scattered knowledge of psychology they already have in their repertoire. It is fascinating to contemplate how, even if only superficially, Freudian modes of thinking have slipped into popular culture. Even without having read any of Freud's work s, all students know something about his thinking, though their opinions of him will not necessarily be positive. Some will find the essay to be valuable in teaching the individual something about his needs/motives and generally sensible in the examples used. Students argue less about what Freud calls the manifest content of the dream than about the latent content, and that is clearly a way into thinking about literary analysis, with the dream analogous to the text.

Metaphors: Most students will probably agree that although dreams are difficult to understand, they do indeed offer some meaning for a part of existence that some people use in a variety of ways. This serious approach to dreams has a long history in the Judeo-Christian tradition, as in the Biblical story of Joseph's interpretation of the Pharaoh's dream which saved Egypt from famine. But the importance of Freud as a major maker of twentieth-century culture is that he started to give us a way of probing those sources of behavior and patterns of choice that lay beneath the surface and which are revealed, however indirectly, in dreams.

A very fruitful way of teaching Freud is to use the common post-structuralist analysis between dream and meaning, dream-text and literary text. Readers of literary texts are like analysts, probing texts for significances below the level of the obvious; similarly, we all probe the complex surface of our own society for meanings—for what Fredric Jameson terms the "political" unconscious.

GEORGE ORWELL, "POLITICS AND THE ENGLISH LANGUAGE"

Response Statement Assignments

1. Orwell says that it is "clear that the decline of a language must ultimately have political and economic causes." What in your literary or political repertoire prepares you for this theory about the relationship between language and civilization? Do you find Orwell's argument persuasive? Do you agree that a sloppy approach to language reflects a careless approach to ethics and morality? How do you feel about your own language patterns?

2. How do you respond to the style of this essay? Would you like to have an English teacher who spoke and thought like Orwell?

Teaching Notes

Literary and Political Repertoire: For most of our students, unless they have read and discussed the Williams or the Harris essays, Orwell's ideas in this essay may well be surprising, for they may have never thought of political/social/economic decline as being in any way related to the way people speak. Students need to be encouraged to explore further how all aspects of society interact.

Orwell's argument may seem excessively moralistic to some. Others may agree that writing ought to be clearer, less obtuse, and more accurate, not filled with "dying metaphors." They will also agree with Orwell's condemnation of pretentious diction or meaningless words. What may bother or confuse them is his argument for the connections between language and political and economic decline.

We ask students if they can relate Orwell's arguments to other texts, asking such questions as: Do you think that the leaders of nations communicate with each other in precise and concise language? How do you feel about the language of the media? Do you feel that all educated people should use language in the same ways? Can standard use of language be possible in a large multi-ethnic country like the United States where so many regional dialects exist? Do you think that Orwell is saying that language should never change, or that it should be kept pure? How can you really define a "decline" in language or place a value judgment on how it is used? As you grapple with such questions, students will recognize that since relationships between language and culture do exist, perhaps carelessness in one area provokes carelessness in another.

Prose Style: Some of your students who have read Animal Farm will be surprised to discover that George Orwell wrote this essay, since it seems so academic. A few students will have read 1984 and talk about its tone and message--fearful, violent, prophesizing a mechanical and controlled society. You might ask students who have read either book to bring sections to read in class that seem to parallel some of Orwell's ideas in the essay. Many students will find the arguments in Animal Farm and 1984, though not dissimilar to those of the essay, to be more convincing because they are presented in the fictional form. This can again provoke interesting discussions about the relationship between "fact" and "fiction."

ROLAND BARTHES, "THE PHOTOGRAPHIC MESSAGE"

Response Statement Assignments

1. How do you respond to Barthes's concept of the way in which viewers fill in gaps when they view what appears to be a realistic photograph? When you have looked, for example, at photos of fires, or other kinds of disasters in the newspaper, have you thought about how much of your own repertoire you bring to those pictures? Why do you think that Barthes chooses the photograph to make his point? Does using the photograph, as opposed to the painting, help make his point better?

2. Do you agree with Barthes's argument that the visual image cannot stand alone and must interact with a verbal message, whether on the page of a newspaper or in the mind of the viewer? Could you respond to a photograph with a strong political or feminist reading, perhaps a religious reading, which had no accompanying caption? How about one that had a photographic message and caption which conflicted sharply with attitudes of your own? How are responses such as these possible?

Teaching Notes

Repertoire and Viewer's Inferencing: This is a seminal essay and clearly connects with others among the selections, especially Masters's and Harris's. Ask your students why they feel that Barthes uses photographs in order to make his point about the importance of context. Some of them will argue that photographs seem to be the most objective and accurate form of communication we have ("the camera never lies"), though students interested in photography disagree. They will point out that the photographer makes many decisions that influence what is seen: angle of vision, what is shown and not shown, distance from the subject, and so on. Ask such students if these same considerations would be true of a photographer taking pictures of a disaster, who has no time for making such decisions. Some will realize that there is always time for a decision and that the pictures the photographer takes are always the product of some repertoire and are always influenced by the medium itself. All the still photographs we see, of course, have been developed and printed, and often cropped, by specialists who seek to have them express certain messages as strongly and clearly as possible. What is more, the ones we see in the media have been selected--with others being discarded--by editors and authors who have stories in mind that the photos are supposed to illustrate. Ideologically loaded choices are found even in seemingly technical matters. Students who know something of journalism or publishing will point out how these processes can use a supposedly "objective" photo to generate an artistic, political, or social effect. We then discuss the photograph as an interaction of the photographer's and editor's attitudes, the language of the text that surrounds the picture, and the viewer's repertoire.

Visual and Verbal Interaction: You can also use this essay to introduce the concept, if you have not done so before, of the signifier and the signified, which apply to discussions of how the photograph and context interact to provide meaning. A photograph, like a word, can have a connotative meaning depending on how it is used, and you might look at some examples that Barthes provides in the text of the essay. Students can then see how it is possible to bring strong readings, feminist, political, religious, and others, to a photograph. When they bring in some of their own examples, they argue about interpretations, justifying their arguments by explaining the strategies they used. You might also discuss some cross-cultural readings. How would a person in the third world "read" a photograph of people being fed in soup kitchens in New York City, in the same way as an affluent American or an official Soviet journalist? How differently would these people read fashion photos or photographs of riots in South Africa?

JOHN F. KENNEDY, "INAUGURAL ADDRESS"

Response Statement Assignments

1. How do you respond to this address? Are your assumptions about what a political speech should be confirmed or challenged by reading this address?

2. Do you respond to this speech with some emotion? What in your repertoire evokes that emotion? Kennedy's violent death? The entire Kennedy family? The war in Vietnam? Kennedy's wife? His brothers, especially Robert who was also killed, and Edward who remains in the political arena despite the scandals that touched his life?

Teaching Notes

Assumptions and a Political Reading: With this and with King's speech, you can deeply analyze what your students bring to their hearing or reading of a political speech. Their responses will include criticism of generalities, since political leaders tend not to be too specific about issues; the patriotic flavor of a political speech; the attempt to influence people, not so much by what is said, but by how. (You might get a tape of Kennedy's or King's speech and ask students to contrast their different effects when heard as opposed to read.)

Why do political speeches deal with general issues rather than with specific stands on issues? Or should you rather listen to tone: "Do I like the person who is talking?" Most students will feel that the Kennedy "Inaugural Address," though less immediately "political" (in the popular sense) in that it was intended to pull people together after an election, has many expected elements: the pledge, comments on a variety of topical subjects, the calling on God--rhetorical elements that generally move listeners powerfully. All of these are no less ideologically loaded--indeed, it is at the level of the general that ideology is at its most visible.

History and Repertoire: Most of your students will probably feel that it is difficult to separate Kennedy from his personal history and from the history of his family. Those students, who according to their peers believe in the Kennedy myth, will be moved by both the address and by the sense that Kennedy had the potential to make a great difference on our country. Others, who do not share a positive sense of the Kennedy years, will not be so moved. Help your students analyze the ways in which the repertoires they brought to this speech made a significant difference in how they responded to it.

RAYMOND WILLIAMS, "KEYWORDS" (Selection)

Response Statement Assignments

1. Choose another "keyword," one that you find is loaded with changing, contradictory values. Use the Oxford English Dictionary to write your own "keyword" entry.

2. What reading strategies did you find most useful in your approach to the Williams essay? Why did you use the strategy or strategies you chose?

Teaching Notes

History: Most students find Williams's information about how the meanings of specific words have changed to be interesting. Students can easily follow his argument about how words like "consumer" developed connotative meanings over time. When they attempt to do some research in the history of language to discover if they can develop keywords of their own, discussions can become even more provocative. One of the exercises we've used consistently with success is to get students to put together a kind of supplement to Williams's book. The words "feminist" and "feminine" stirred some disagreement about what they have come to suggest, and how, in fact, they are different--"feminine" sometimes being considered an insult to a feminist. We find that students write a good argument by starting with a word, doing some research, and then developing the meaning of the word both historically and culturally. The OED is a valuable tool here--and such an excuse is an excellent way of introducing students to library research.

Perhaps the most important points to convey about the Keywords extracts are that:

1. Language simultaneously reflects and influences

2. Language is always a site of struggle between a society's conflicting and contradictory values

3. Language changes, as well, historically, and the history of words records the changing battles between rival ideologies

You will find a more detailed treatment of these points in Chapter 2 of Reading Texts.

MICHEL FOUCAULT, "THE ORDER OF THINGS"

Response Statement Assignments

1. How do you respond to the division of animals into the categories of the "Chinese encyclopedia" reported by Borges? What does that division suggest to you about your own society's ways of categorizing things? Do you find Foucault's essay to be unsettling? amusing? strange?

2. Do you perceive experience as chaotic? How do you define "order"? In what ways does Foucault challenge those expectations? How do you regard the ways in which people impose systems of order on the chaos of experience?

Teaching Notes

Repertoire: Take students more slowly through the Foucault essay because they may at first find it difficult to read. As in readings of the essay in general, we remind students to look first at surface meaning and then at perspectives, their own and that of the author. Here we may suggest that they look carefully, before writing a response, at the section on the division of animals. What they perceive is that the encyclopedia sees outer or obvious peculiarities of things as those that give them their essential identities. That is the system of the encyclopedia, its way of ordering the world. We then discuss the ways in which students tend to order their world according to individual repertoires—religious, social, economic, political.

Language and Culture: If students have read the Barthes, Orwell, or Harris essays, they will be familiar with the ways in which language and culture interact: that language reflects culture while culture defines language, both in patterns and in meaning. People in very cold climates have many names for snow because it is so important to their lives; we have many names for business situations in our culture because of their significance to us. Students will also understand the distinction between connotative and denotative meanings from discussions of poetry and from Barthes's essay. Thus they should have less difficulty in understanding what Foucault means by the chaos of experience and systems of order. What makes discussions especially interesting are students' personal comments about how they use language to impose order on their own lives. Since they feel a lack of control over what might happen, they use a whole variety of strategies to impose order—prayers, compulsive speech patterns, calling parents or friends if they feel vulnerable, talking about one thing to forget concerns about another. Religious students tend to see less chaos in life, but might find it difficult to recognize that it is the carefully selective (or restrictive) faith that helps them to reduce the confusion they might otherwise see around them. We probably engage in some form of categorization every minute of our lives. We do it with people who remind us of other people, and engage in stereotypical thinking because of our need to impose order.

MARTIN LUTHER KING, JR., "I HAVE A DREAM"

Response Statement Assignments

1. How do you respond to the speech's treatment of problems of racial equality and prejudice? Does it make you want to act or join in as one of the group listening to the speech, or do you read it as a part of history?

2. What do you think is the basis of the appeal of this speech? Do you respond with more emotion to this speech, to fiction you have read about racial injustice, or to the play A Raisin in the Sun?

Teaching Notes

History and a Political Reading: Many students may admit the rhetorical power of King's speech but tend to find its message somewhat dated. Some will feel that much has changed since this speech was given; others will feel that what King asks for is too general and does not go far enough in asking for change. Some of the latter may think that a modern leader would tie up his/her speech with blacks all over the world, and with the suffering in third-world countries. Others will undoubtedly insist that the speech still has important political implications and can stir up their feelings. Almost all students will agree with the power of King's language, with its emotion, repetition, the almost "poetic" quality of the prose. Some students may talk about hearing King's voice as they read the speech. Here, as we move away from the issue of history, we want our students to talk about the sources of rhetorical power, the emotion-laden subject, the way the narrative of the essay moves forward, the use of metaphor and simple language.

Literary Repertoire: Here we sometimes try to compare the various genres in their effectiveness in moving reader's emotions. Many students will agree that King's speech is so much more rousing than most political speeches they hear, and that they would love to make an argument like King's. Ask them whether they nevertheless find themselves more moved by fiction and drama. This again raises the questions of the rhetorical power of fact over fiction or vice versa. Some will feel that the specific illustrations of injustice in fiction and drama involve the reader more effectively. Thus in A Raisin in the Sun or "Like A Winding Sheet" they meet the people, they live with the situations, they become more involved.

SUSAN SONTAG, "ILLNESS AS METAPHOR"

Response Statement Assignments

1. What is your response to Sontag's distinction between TB and cancer? Do you view tuberculosis as romantic, as an illness from which people died as they do in opera, looking beautiful, just flushed a little from fever? Do you view cancer as a "disease that doesn't knock before it enters...an illness experienced as a ruthless, secret invasion..."? Is cancer something to be kept secret? Would it be kept a secret in your family, as Sontag predicts?

2. Susan Sontag has had a long bout with cancer, with special treatments, pain, and the expected problems that accompany the disease when doctors try to keep it under control. So far, she seems to be in remission. Does adding that information to your repertoire change your feelings about the essay?

Teaching Notes

Illness as Metaphor: Students probably find Sontag's argument a new way of looking at how metaphors exist in society. Talk about cancer as a metaphor and compare that with the way in which they view tuberculosis, no longer the threat it once was. You can raise a number of questions such as: How does cancer, the word, become the name for an illness and how does that name characterize that illness in the language? Do you associate tuberculosis, as Sontag sees it, with romantic illness and death, or with pain and suffering? Do you agree that the mention of cancer produces fear, secrecy, shame? Do you agree with Sontag's argument that cancer produces these reactions because of the parts of the body that become diseased? Students can be deeply affected by these questions, especially those who have had personal experience with the illness, with someone in their family or with a friend. Some of our students agree with Sontag's metaphor but they add that much of the fear and secrecy stems from not wanting an invalid to know that he/she is dying. Others feel that Sontag's definition of the metaphor is dated, and that cancer is no longer regarded with such secrecy, noting that President Reagan's operation for cancer was openly discussed in the press. Some talk about cancer in their own families, of successful treatments, optimistic concern, and courage. A few students may mention a generational difference and say that their grandparents retain fears such as Sontag described, even fears of contagion, but that they and their parents don't.

Repertoire: Most of our students respond with some emotion to our telling them about Sontag's battle with cancer. The AIDS parallel is an obvious one to draw--an interesting project is to try to extend Sontag's argument and see what metaphors are commonly used for this disease.

A Sample Syllabus with Teaching Notes and Writing Assignments

The syllabus is divided into five modules or parts as follows.

1. Enjoying Reading and Responding to Literature

2. Factors Influencing Responses: Language, History, Culture

3. Reading in History

4. The Role of Sign Systems in Constituting Us as Thinking Subjects in Our Culture

5. The Implications of Becoming Conscious of How Language, History, and Culture Influence Our Readings

There are a number of subsections under each of these modules which can be cut or shortened as appropriate. The length of these modules is obviously flexible and can be adapted to a semester of varying length. Note, too, that we specify many texts from which you can choose!

As we say to our instructors, we don't expect or want you to teach all of this stuff! But we do want the five major issues that organize the course to be raised. The following itemized requirements and explanation are addressed to students; they may of course be adapted as needed.

Required Texts

The Lexington Introduction to Literature

Reading Texts (optional)

Suggested Course Requirements

1. Regular Response Statements   (35% of grade)
2. Three papers, including one research paper   (50% of grade)
3. Class participation   (15% of grade)

Outline of Course

This course gives priority to analyzing your interactions with texts rather than to texts in themselves. In this class, we will regard meaning as something that readers create with a text rather than as something they find in texts. We will study reading as a culturally-acquired process, and we will examine, through writing assignments, the interaction of the processes of reading and writing.

Our primary goal is to enjoy reading and writing about literature. But it is also to understand these complex processes. We will analyze various factors--linguistic, historical, and cultural--that contribute to the ways in which you read. In studying how you respond to literary texts, we will address such issues as how the "meanings" of the "same" text can change over time, why different kinds of texts seem to demand different kinds of readers (i.e., do you read a poem differently from the way you read a novel?), whether the author of a work can be considered its final "authority," and, perhaps most important, what the social and political implications are of becoming conscious of the factors influencing the ways you read and interpret.

To help you address such questions as these, you must keep a written record of your responses to each reading. These are called **response statements**. Generally, in the first part of the response statement, you will discuss the particular effects reading a text had on you. In the second part, you will explore the reasons why you think the text had that effect, focusing on both what the text and the reader bring to the reading.

Response statements are not research or formal essays; they can be written in a casual style (but they must make sense!), and they can be handwritten so long as they are neat. They are a way of helping you to become conscious of various factors influencing your responses to texts and become accustomed to writing about those responses. As the semester progresses, we will examine how you can use various strategies to write response statements, how you can expand your initial responses, and how (a major goal!) you can become a **strong reader**.

You will learn, too, to write a more formal paper, though it will incorporate, not abandon, the kinds of insights in the reading experience that you will have acquired from your response statements. You will also be introduced to a number of important concepts, such as **repertoire** and **ideology**. You should, whenever necessary, consult the glossary in the Lexington Introduction to Literature, and pay particular attention to the Introductions there, parts of which will be regularly assigned for class discussion.

PART I: ENJOYING READING AND RESPONDING TO LITERATURE

A. Introduction and discussion of general aims of course

1. Sit in a circle. Introduce yourself. Give a short discussion of course goals, that is, this is a reader- and culture-centered course which encourages students to become conscious of how and why they respond as they do to texts of all kinds, and tries to develop them into cognitively and culturally aware strong readers.

2. Devise an **interesting and funny example** that will involve the class in order to illustrate the many factors influencing interpretation and the inability of anyone to have access to "objective" knowledge. For example, assume that we're all having a party and one person appears to trip over his/her <u>Lexington Introduction</u> and spills a drink on another person's shirt. What <u>really</u> happened? Allow students to make up explanations themselves. Examples: one student will contend that the act was intentional because he knows something about the "drink spiller." Another says it was not intentional because the drink spiller is always tripping over something and is otherwise a nice guy. A third student will confess that she did not really see the event, but assumes that the spiller was tripped by the person standing next to him whom she doesn't like, etc. Let this go on for about 10 minutes or so, encouraging students to come up with as imaginative interpretations as possible.

3. Analyze the factors influencing students' interpretations:

Such factors include:

- prior knowledge of people involved

- level of interest and attention

- awareness of party conventions, and conventional notions of "normal" or "appropriate" behavior

- emotional identification with one of the people involved

4. Gently suggest that these and other similar factors influence people's responses to literature—as well as to everything else in any interpretive situation.

5. Discuss response statements. Make it clear that response statements are graded somewhat differently from more formal papers—on clarity, imagination, detail, and self-awareness. Most response statements are graded only by a check, check +, or check −, but at least eight selected statements are given letter grades, the sum of which will count as 35% of grade. Hand out the following guidelines for writing response statements.

GUIDELINES FOR RECORDING RESPONSES TO TEXTS

- **What Is the Initial Predominant Effect of the Text on You?** confusion, suspense, identification with characters, interest, boredom, amusement, terror, etc. Expand as much as possible.

- **Why Do You Think the Text Had That Effect?** To answer this you should examine:

- The nature of the text: subject matter, language, structure, use of familiar/unfamiliar conventions, organization, social norms, characters, themes, gaps or blanks in the structure which reader has to fill in, etc.

- The nature of the reader: Did you have prior knowledge of or expectations about the text or about literature in general? What were your reading patterns (consistency-building/wandering viewpoint)? Did you have knowledge/lack of knowledge about particular literary or social conventions? Did you have knowledge/lack of knowledge about historical period?

- **What Does Your Response Tell You About Yourself?** About your style of reading, about assumptions you hold regarding literature, our society, our codes of behavior, your notion of what is "normal," etc.

6. Go over syllabus.

7. Give students a selection of modern poetry and assign response statement:

Choose the two poems you like best and answer the question on the response statement sheet explaining why you like these poems.

This response statement should be handed in during the next class. We suggest the following poems are suitable:

Thomas, "Do Not Go Gentle into that Good Night"
    (strategies; general repertoire)
Reed, "beware : do not read this poem"
    (very popular with students--great intro to strategies,
    expectations, and gaps)
Roethke, "My Papa's Waltz" (gaps, emotional identification)
Daniels, "At a Poetry Reading" (general and literary
    repertoire, gaps)
Ferlinghetti, "Underwear" (repertoire, "what is poetry?")
Frost, "The Road Not Taken" (gaps, emotional identification)

B. What Do You Like?

1. Select a wide variety of poems such as the above for students to write a response statement on and to read for the next class meeting(s). Criteria for your selection: at least some of the poems should be fairly easy to understand; some should be humorous; all, in one way or another, should illustrate concepts such as intertextuality, gaps, repertoire, strategies, consistency building/wandering viewpoint, active/passive reading styles, possibilities for strong reading, ideology, etc. (Note that we marked above what particular concepts can most easily be introduced with particular poems. We do not expect you to give students these notations.) These concepts can be gently introduced <u>after</u> students have already responded enthusiastically to the poems and explained their reading strategies-- the theoretical vocabulary is meant to enhance students' understanding of their own responses, not to be a barrier to it. Go with the flow--probably only 2-4 poems will be discussed and students should decide what they'll be. As concepts come up, refer students to appropriate sections in introductions.

2. After 2-4 poems have been discussed, ask students to summarize factors influencing their likes and dislikes. Possible factors:

• understandability

• subject matter

- having learned something

- humor

- interesting language

- confirming/defying expectations

- aesthetic pleasure

- emotional identification

- shared (or different) ideology

3. Assign the relevant parts of the Poetry Introduction, especially the part that deals with the enjoyment of poetry. You may want to discuss the ideas in class. Then assign the same response statement for a new set of poems, including those from other periods. Encourage use of newly learned vocabulary in response statements.

C. Why Do You Like What You Like? What Is Your Literary Repertoire?

1. Assign the following:

Plath, "Lady Lazarus"
Pound, "In a Station of the Metro"
Williams, "This Is Just to Say"
Blake, "The Lamb"
Atwood, "You Fit into Me"
Dickinson, "Because I Could Not Stop for Death"
Wordsworth, "I Wandered Lonely as a Cloud"

2. Focus on getting students comfortable with new vocabulary when they talk about poems. Feel free to let them talk about poems from previous class as well as this class.

3. Introduce the notion that **poetry is as much a way of reading as a way of writing** and encourage students to become increasingly analytical about their reading strategies.

4. Assign reading for the first (theoretical) lesson in Part II (opening sections of General Introduction).

Response statement assignment to begin Part II:

Compare and contrast your reading strategies and responses to Maupassant, "Miss Harriet," and Atwood, "Loulou: Or, The Domestic Life of the Language," taking into account: (a) the different narrative techniques of the two stories; (b) the different time periods and cultures in which the stories were written; (c) your historical situation (cultural norms, historical values, and social/sexual stereotypes); (d) your gender.

D. Theoretical Lesson

To conclude this first part, reinforce some of the theoretical points. Study the opening sections of General Introduction, "Becoming a Strong Reader."

PART II: INTRODUCTION TO VARIOUS FACTORS INFLUENCING RESPONSE: LANGUAGE, HISTORY, CULTURE

Instructors may find it useful to consult Chapter Two of Reading Texts by Kathleen McCormick, Gary Waller, and Linda Flower (D.C. Heath, 1987) on the Language–History–Culture triad.

A. How Do Different Conventions of Storytelling Create Different Strategies of Reading? How Do the Reader's and Text's Historical Situation and the Reader's Gender Affect Response?

> Munro, "Lives of Girls and Women"
> Chopin, "Regret"
> Maupassant, "Miss Harriet"
> Atwood, "Loulou; or, The Domestic Life of the Language"
> A selection of poems by and about women from the sixteenth century onwards (e.g. by Sidney, Donne, Shakespeare, Marvell, Bradstreet, Pope, Wordsworth, Keats, Barrett Browning, Dickinson, Rossetti, Plath, Sexton, Rich, Bishop, etc.)
> Harris, "Women, Baseball, and Words"

The Response Statement Assignment on Maupassant and Atwood given at the end of the previous section can be discussed here. (It can also, of course, be used with other texts in this selection.)

Part II of the syllabus should gently introduce students to the ways in which **language, history,** and **culture** influence their reading, and how in order to become strong readers they should start to ask wider questions, related to their culture, rather than just what is "in" the text. To introduce this module, allow students to respond freely to the stories and you, as teacher, provide the terminology for clarifying and analyzing their responses as the occasion arises.

1. Before talking about the two stories written about in students' response statements, read a couple of response statements from previous classes, one that is clear, one that is vague, in order to give students a sense of criteria. Continue to do this on a fairly regular basis throughout the course, but particularly in the beginning, to highlight what a good response statement is, to reinforce points made in the classes, perhaps to gently introduce a bright, but quiet student into the class discussion, to make connections between the previous class and the current class, etc.

2. Analyze the differences in points of view of the stories. Students may object to sexism (male or female) in one or the other story. (language and culture)

3. Allow students to characterize the various styles of storytelling and the differences these create in response. Some will find Atwood's style psychologically more realistic than Maupassant's; others will be annoyed with the way Atwood seems to direct them to see things from a "feminist" viewpoint. These are good examples, for those students who think that meaning is contained in the text, of how the same textual strategies cause different responses in different readers. (language and literary ideology)

4. Many students find Atwood's main character tiresome and weak--others may see class antagonism rather than a gender-specific one between Loulou and her men. Some will find Maupassant's story more dated, some more "timeless," despite the fact that its sexual norms are dated. The introduction of gender-related questions may or may not worry students--some will think the "women's movement" dated, others that it is not yet dominant enough. This can lead to a discussion of how relations between the sexes have changed over history. (history and culture)

5. Discuss poems by and about women from the <u>Lexington</u> <u>Introduction</u> and ask students to analyze the cultural norms or repertoires implicit in these poems. What are the attitudes of the speaker to the world, to men, to herself? How directly does she address the subjects of her poems? How do the pronouns "I" and "you" shift within and between poems? Try to get students to establish some of the differences in the poems' uses of language before they address more generally the various cultural attitudes toward women--otherwise students may try to avoid talking about the poems altogether because they are difficult to understand. They should perhaps also read the Harris essay, "Women, Baseball, and Words."

Analyze the ways in which attitudes toward women have changed in the last three centuries. Students are aware of the women's movement and of many obvious changing roles of women in society (women work, live alone, ask men out, demand "equal rights"), so this part of the discussion can initially proceed quite quickly. What will often take longer to establish is that any historical period contains many conflicts, some over social roles, and that, therefore, one cannot simply say that women were thought of as X in the 1600s and Y in the 1900s. An effective way of introducing this notion is to try to establish in students a sense of their <u>own</u> historical situatedness—some students, for example, will feel that women have achieved their goals and that militant or organized feminism is or should be a thing of the past; others will feel that sexism is on the rise in the 80s and that women must be active feminists to avoid falling back into stereotypical roles. What this illustrates is that in any period, including the Renaissance, Victorian era, or today, ideas about any subject are always in conflict and are seldom clearly defined.

After students have realized that one cannot oversimplify any historical period, return to some of the poems and look for more conflicts in them, for ways in which they differ from themselves, for ways in which the subject of the poem is often split.

6. Assign as a response statement for the following class on Stein and Poe the following:

Explain your responses to Stein's "As a Wife Has a Cow" and Poe's "The Cask of Amontillado," taking into account: a) the strategies you used to read the stories (wandering viewpoint, consistency-building, filling in gaps); b) your knowledge and expectations of the authors or the type of stories they write; c) the strategies used in each story; d) the repertoire of the stories. If you do not have any knowledge of Stein's work, record your initial response to "As a Wife," and then go to the library to find out some information about Stein's goals as a writer, the influences on her work, and the general reception of her work. Explain how and whether gaining further information about Stein's work changes the ways in which you respond to it.

<u>Some explanatory material you might use</u>: You should assign the relevant parts of the fiction introduction here, especially on the use of reading strategies. If necessary, discuss them in class. Explain to students that the same textual strategies cause different responses in different readers. Thus, their responses have as much to do with them as with the text. The point of their analysis is to explain <u>why</u> they had the responses they did (they can no longer attribute them solely to the text if responses among them differ). For example, instead of their saying "X makes no sense," or "X is clear," or "X is unrealistic," ask students to explain what their notion of making sense, being clear, being unrealistic, etc., is. They should be graded on their ability to analyze the factors influencing their responses.

B. How Do the Reader's Expectations and Level of Expertise Affect Response?

Poe, "The Cask of Amontillado"
Stein, "As a Wife Has a Cow"

The goal of the classes dealing with this section is to help students recognize that their background as well as the strategies of the stories themselves contribute to their very different effects on readers. The focus, therefore, is on language, especially as a part of culture, i.e., how students have been educated by their educational institutions and by society at large to define "a good or interesting story."

1. Focus on the different strategies readers adopted in reading the two stories. Students will frequently argue about whether they read Poe in an active or a passive way, but almost all will agree that they didn't know how to read Stein. A few, however, will generally enjoy "As a Wife," finding that they like the rhythms of the language or that it reads more like poetry to them, etc. These students seem to have a greater tolerance for ambiguity and are more comfortable with a wandering viewpoint. Emphasize that different students react in diverse ways to texts because they read them in different ways. Probe students to discover why they read the way they do; emphasize that reading strategies are acquired, not natural.

2. Presumably "As a Wife" will be disorienting—analyze the expectations students have about language and stories that make the story difficult for them. From a discussion such as this, students will realize that they do have an literary repertoire (for example, they may expect stories to have a clear beginning, middle, and end; they expect a plot, a theme, and character development—all characteristics of Poe's story).

3. Analyze students' different degrees of preparedness for the two stories—most have read stories by Poe previously or at least are familiar with the conventions of suspense stories. Fewer are familiar with Stein! Analyze how gaining information on Stein's artistic goals and cubist influences may change the way students react to "As a Wife"; emphasize that students' repertoires of knowledge greatly influence the ways in which they react to texts. Reintroduce differences between naive and expert readers by pointing out that increased information often helps one to naturalize a text.

C. How Do Changing Cultural Attitudes Influence the Creation and the Reading of Texts?

1. The focus of these classes is on culture, and to a lesser extent on language. The goal of these classes is to introduce students to the notion, not only that writers and readers are influenced by the culture in which they live, but that any culture, and, therefore, any writer, reader, or text is written by multiple discourses. You can do this in many different ways. One we recommend is to

take the interconnected concepts of **ideology** and **general repertoire**. Refer to the diagram in "Becoming a Strong Reader" and have a discussion on **ideology** and how it operates in any society. It defines not a set of ideas we disapprove of but, more neutrally, the assumptions and seemingly natural pattern of life of any society. It provides the values of a society that are, more or less, taken for granted by members of that society. For your own purposes (and for students taking a post-freshman literature course) we recommend studying as well Reading Texts, Chapters 1 and 2.

Then take a selection of modern poems and perhaps (if you are spreading this Part of the syllabus out a little) Death of a Salesman. As we explain in the Drama Introduction, it is an excellent text for getting students to discuss some of the dominant ideological assumptions of twentieth-century America. See the Teaching Notes on Miller's play as well.

If students find the poems rather difficult to understand, some close reading is in order; the focus of the reading, however, should not be on developing a summary, or a consensus interpretation, but rather should embrace multiple and often contradictory interpretations afforded by the poetry. There is, as we note in discussing Miller's play, an excellent selection of videotaped productions.

2. In preparation for the next part of the course, have students read Kafka's "The Metamorphosis" and Calvino's "The Canary Prince," and prepare to write the following paper:

Compare and contrast your reading strategies, responses, and interpretations of these stories. Develop a clear thesis that explains the various factors, such as expectations, familiarity with different conventions of storytelling, etc., that help you to decide how to read, analyze, and interpret these stories. How did you learn to have certain expectations and to understand certain storytelling conventions?

Point out that in both stories, for example, metamorphoses occur. Do students respond in similar or different ways to them? Why? Have students demonstrate with specific examples how they read certain passages of each story and why they read them in that way. Did they, for example, feel "compelled" to ask certain questions of Kafka's story that they did not ask of Calvino's and vice versa. Why/Why not?

Emphasize to students that the source of their responses to texts lies not so much "in" the texts as in how they have been trained by their education and society generally to read texts. Because responses among them will differ, they cannot explain their responses by means of "the text"; the text, as we have seen, is not an objective thing; it does not "contain" a single meaning. It is produced by the culturally-conditioned expectations and assumptions they bring to bear when reading it.

Further, point out to students that they need not choose which story they like better (the stories are so different that this may be difficult anyway). Students will be graded on their ability both to describe clearly their responses and to analyze the factors influencing their responses.

3. Then, as a first step towards the formal paper, assign as a <u>response</u> statement on "The Canary Prince" and "The Metamorphosis" the following:

A. What kinds of textual strategies/conventions indicate the genre of "The Canary Prince?" When in the story do you realize what genre it is? What kinds of expectations do you have about how the story will develop and end? How does your knowledge of the strategies of writing stories of this kind affect the strategies you use to read them? What kinds of questions do you not ask about the story? (List three.)

B. What kinds of questions do you ask of "The Metamorphosis?" By what processes do you go about interpreting it? What textual strategies and what expectations or assumptions of yours influence the way you respond to this story?

D. The Process of Developing an Interpretation: How Do You Move from Response Statements to a Formal Paper? How Do You Determine What Your Literary Ideology Is and What Cultural Forces Help to Shape It?

Calvino, "The Canary Prince"
Kafka, "The Metamorphosis"

The first purpose of these classes is to allow students to talk freely about their responses to the two texts, but only minimally about the factors influencing those responses, which is the subject of their paper topic. The second purpose is to explain clearly the differences between a response statement and a more formal paper.

1. The students should direct most of the discussion of these stories, with minimal guidance by the teacher. They should have been asked to read in advance the relevant parts of the Fiction Introduction, and you might want to discuss them in class. Students, for example, will probably be comfortable with the metamorphosis of the Canary Prince but not with that of Gregor. They probably will not ask whether the prince and princess are compatible or why the king is so shortsighted, but on the other hand, they will analyze the family relationships of the Samsas. They will not "identify" with the characters in "The Canary Prince," but they frequently identify with Gregor. They will often decide that Gregor's metamorphosis, unlike the Canary Prince's, is psychological. Remind students frequently that they must analyze the institutional, cultural, and aesthetic factors underlying these responses, but don't discuss them in class in any detail.

In their papers, students should draw on their experiences in the course thus far to help them analyze their reactions to the stories: the significance of gaps and storytelling conventions, the matching of the repertoire of the text with the repertoire of the reader, the institutional sources of their expectations about stories and, in this case, metamorphoses, the capacity of a subject--the Prince or Gregor--to differ from himself. You will expect students, for example, to discuss the different settings in which they were introduced to these two kinds of stories and how these settings influenced their reading strategies: fairy tales in childhood where the distinction between imagination and reality is blurred; realistic stories in English classes where, if something out of the ordinary occurs, it is frequently regarded as symbolic so that it can be naturalized by the reader. The best students will recognize that, with different genre expectations, they might have analyzed the fairy tale symbolically and accepted Gregor's metamorphosis as normal.

2. Establish differences between response statements and formal papers. Discuss the function of a thesis paragraph. Provide reasons to avoid excessive amounts of colloquial writing in papers. Emphasize that papers must have a sense of audience—while a response statement is often quite introspective, a paper must be aware of its readers—be clear, interesting, persuasive. Discuss the importance of revision, not just editing after a first draft is written. See Chapter 4 in Reading Texts for a detailed analysis of the similarities and differences between a response statement and a formal paper, and for a discussion of the ways in which the writing of formal papers must change once students have written culturally-aware response statements.

3. Assign as the next response statement on love poetry to prepare for Part III the following:

Compare and contrast your reactions to Petrarchan and Elizabethan love sonnets with your reactions to carpe diem poems. Did you like/dislike this poetry? Why?

In trying to explain your reactions, explore:

A. The historical/cultural differences between the 1980s and the time in which the poetry was written.

B. The role your gender plays in your liking/disliking the poetry.

C. The way you react to the language, metaphors, and sexual attitudes of the poems.

D. Whether any of the metaphors or attitudes in these poems seem familiar to you. If so, from what contemporary sources? If anything seems familiar, does this contribute to your liking or disliking the poetry?

You should also assign the relevant parts of the Poetry Introduction for reference, especially the reading of the Wyatt poem.

PART III: READING IN HISTORY

A. How Do Changing Values Affect the History of Texts' Receptions? Can We Specify the Dominant Discourse of Any Culture? What Makes a Text Seem "Original"? What Makes a Text Seem "Conventional"?

1. Focus on different responses to Petrarchan and Elizabethan love poetry and carpe diem poetry:

> Sidney, "Sonnet 52"
> Shakespeare, "Sonnets"
> Herrick, "To the Virgins"
> Waller, "Go, Lovely Rose"
> Lovelace, "To Althea, from Prison"
> Jonson, "Song: To Celia"
> Marvell, "To His Coy Mistress"

Allow students not only to respond honestly to the poems (most of them will initially not like the Petrarchan and Elizabethan sonnets), but especially to articulate clearly the reasons why they like or do not like these poems. Such an exercise will help students to explore the interaction between literary and general repertoires. For example, many may think that these love sonnets are boring or artificial--they have often read them in high school English classes and were told to appreciate them (institutional pressure) when often they really didn't like or understand them. Probe students to discover why they like or do not like this poetry. Some of their reasons will have to do with literary ideology-- flowery language, etc.; others reasons will be more social and political in nature--the women are sexual objects, the men are sexually subjugated, etc. (The discussion of the Wyatt poem in the Poetry Introduction can be gone over carefully at this point.) You may suggest to students that comments such as these indicate that they possess historical awareness and cultural perspective. These notions can then be the focus of future discussion.

2. Most students will recognize Petrarchanism as the source of many conventions in contemporary advertising, pop songs, and beauty products such as Pearl Drops tooth polish and Silkience shampoo; while most students will accept Petrarchan metaphors in songs and advertising, some will feel that they are cliched, outdated, and sexist in poetry. Suggest to students that such a distinction indicates that they recognize and are written by multiple discourses.

3. Do a close reading of a couple of poems to trace how Petrarchan metaphors work. (Many students do not clearly understand the concept of metaphor until they analyze these poems.) The class should carefully read the section in the Poetry Introduction on Metaphor and Other Figurative Language.

4. When you turn to the carpe diem poems also allow students to respond freely. Most of the women in the class might be insulted by these poems because they perceive the arguments to be ridiculous and condescending (some might even suggest that they now think the Petrarchan sonnets weren't so bad after all!). The men in the class, on the other hand, often report liking carpe diem poems because they "identify" with them, and some actually wonder if women might not find the arguments of these poems to be plausible. The different reactions of the men and women in the class allow you to introduce the notion that these men and women are speaking—and are spoken by— different discourses, some of which are formed by gender difference. These can be teased out and become part of the class discussion.

5. Regardless of their reactions, however, usually both men and women find the carpe diem poems more interesting than Petrarchan sonnets because while the theme of carpe diem poetry may have been integrated into our society, the linguistic wit and comparisons have not. Consequently, this poetry seems fresher, and certainly more shocking to the students, almost all of whom seem to assume that sexual matters were not openly discussed until the twentieth century. Our role in teaching is not to tell students that they are "wrong" to think that Petrarchan poetry is more conventional than carpe diem poetry, which is in fact the older of the two forms. Rather, we should attempt to analyze why students react to the poems in the ways they do and explore the sources from which their notions of conventionality derive. Such an analysis emphasizes the social as well as literary experiences (all of which occur outside students' current reading of these texts) that influence the way readers respond to texts.

6. Do a close reading (focusing on the text strategies) of a couple of poems to trace how the arguments of carpe diem poems work. Explore in depth the cultural and historical forces that have helped to shape students' responses to the poems. Use extracts from response statements as a way into this discussion. Explore more fully the notion that multiple discourses traverse any society. Look not only at students' conflicting responses to a given poem, but at ways in which the poems might differ from themselves, might contradict the ideas about women they seem to be presenting. For example, is the speaker in the carpe diem poems always self-assured; are women in Petrarchan love sonnets always goddesses? Focus on one or two of the more complex poems to begin this discussion, which will reinforce the point that no society or text is ever unified ideologically.

7. Assign the next response statement, on Hamlet, as follows:

    I. Read Hamlet without reading any articles.

        A. What is your opinion of Hamlet?
            —a noble and princely revenger? —cynical and inhuman?
            —delicate and melancholy? —reflective and speculative?

These are just some suggested interpretations; describe Hamlet in your own words. Explain, with reference to the play and to your own assumptions, knowledge, expectations, and reading strategies, why you feel the way you do about Hamlet.

B. Do you think that Hamlet delays excessively in killing Claudius? Why or why not? If you think he does delay excessively, what, in your opinion, are his reasons for doing so?

II. Read a summary of the changing critical views of Hamlet or selections of critical essays on it and answer the following:

A. Do you agree with any/many of the varied, often contradictory interpretations of Hamlet? Have any of these interpretations changed your original opinion of Hamlet or of the problem of his delay?

B. How can you account for so many interpretations of a single play? Is is possible that Freud's theories could apply to a play written in the 17th century? What do all these different interpretations suggest about the status of a text?

C. Are there any constraints on the production of meaning in the text? If you think there are, give examples. Or is meaning determined solely by readers' whims?

For this assignment, have your students read the Hamlet material in the Introduction to Drama, and (if you wish to pursue this question in depth) the John Jump essay, extracts from which you can find in Reading Texts. This essay briefly traces historical trends in Hamlet criticism from the 17th century to the 1960s. Direct your students in addition, perhaps, to Ernest Jones's "Hamlet Diagnosed." This essay gives an explicitly Freudian interpretation of Hamlet in more detail.

B. Why do "Meanings" of the "Same" Text Change Over Time? Can a Text Support Just Any Meaning?

Shakespeare, Hamlet
Stoppard, Rosencrantz and Guildenstern Are Dead

The discussion of Hamlet can be spread over a fair period of time. As the drama introduction in the Lexington Guide points out, Hamlet lends itself admirably to our approach to reading. In these notes, we direct you to some of the most interesting issues it can be used to raise. Bear in mind that you should not spend inordinate amounts of time on plot, character, or theme, nor discussions on developing an interpretation of the play. Most of the students have read the play in high school and have been given a specific interpretation. You should make them aware from the start that your goals are different, and that they are at an advantage for having already read the play. You are concerned with how interpretations develop rather than with developing an interpretation on which they can all agree. That is why the Stoppard play is useful--it is one distinctive modern reading of Hamlet--as well as a fine play in its own right.

1. Elicit students' own reactions to the play. What do they think of Hamlet? Do they think that he is mad? Do they think he delayed excessively in killing Claudius? Although students will disagree in their responses, most will argue that the text did not seem ambiguous to them while they were reading it, i.e., they either thought Hamlet was mad or they didn't, and they did not change their mind while reading. This raises important issues about the nature of students' reading strategies as well as the nature of Hamlet's textual strategies. Why do students seem to be doing so much consistency-building with this particular text? It may have to do with their high school experiences when they were told that a particular interpretation was "correct"; it may have to do with particular assumptions about Shakespeare—contemporary texts can be ambiguous, but a "classic" must be unified, etc. Does the text of Hamlet differ from some of the poetry we've read, or from "As a Wife" or "The Metamorphosis"—texts that seemed ambiguous at the outset?

2. If you are using the Jump article, begin a discussion of the various critics discussed in it. Can students find grounds to agree or disagree with particular positions? If so, what are these grounds? The apparent plausibility of so many interpretations paradoxically supports both the notion that texts constrain interpretation and the notion that they do not. Allow students to introduce the issues of the status of the text and the role of their historical, cultural, and literary assumptions in the creation of meaning, topics that will be discussed in more depth during the next two classes. Concentrate the discussion on Jones's Freudian interpretation of Hamlet. It provides a particularly good focus for analyzing both the influences that critics' assumptions and beliefs have on the criticism they write and the ways in which students' own knowledge affects how they will receive a particular argument. Most students know little or nothing of Freud and reject Jones's interpretation immediately. They often argue that it is somehow incorrect to psychoanalyze a character or that no references to Oedipus exist in the text. Generally, however, a few students learned the Freudian interpretation in high school and fully accept it, and a few will recognize that, given a certain set of assumptions, it could be seen as plausible. This recognition can open up a discussion of the implications of understanding the particular cultural, historical, and literary "paradigms" under which one is operating.

3. After you have introduced to students some issues discussed above about the nature of textual strategies, about the multiple readings of Hamlet that are possible, you will want to focus certain interpretive issues more clearly for students and then open them up for debate:

(a) Do boundary conditions of appropriate response inhere in the text? Allow students to freely debate the issue. Most students are surprised at how little they can say actually exists in the text.

(b) Is there any validity to the distinction "correct/incorrect"? Again, although nearly everybody would like to say "yes," most end up arguing that these distinctions always appear valid, but that they are relative rather than absolute, i.e., what is correct and what is incorrect changes with different assumptions.

(c) How important is the reader's extra-textual knowledge and experiences to the development of an interpretation? It students read Jones, they can now begin to appreciate the need to know more before they can feel comfortable defending a position. This point was introduced in the first classes on poetry (when poems were categorized as "boring" if students didn't understand them) and was reinforced in the class on Stein's "As a Wife," but it becomes more significant here when students see that a piece of criticism, like a literary text, can be completely inaccessible to them if they do not understand its underlying assumptions. Students' recognition that they need information to defend a position or to apprehend a text is not trivial--it can increase their tolerance for ambiguity, their desire to do research, and their willingness to entertain opinions that differ substantially from their own.

(d) What are the implications of recognizing that notions of "truth" are relative? Stoppard's play deals brilliantly with this issue, especially as it provides what is clearly a modern, post-Beckett, perspective on "noble" characters and motives. Students gradually become aware of their historical situatedness. They can start to recognize that whatever they are doing--reading literary texts, buying a new outfit, having a conversation with a friend--they are always thinking and judging within a historical context. This recognition, coupled with their discovery that any society is always traversed by multiple discourses, should give students a sense of freedom rather than one of determinism--and this is an important point to stress in this class. Although we can never escape our historical situatedness, our ideology, we can become more conscious of the underlying assumptions that motivate many of our actions and opinions, and with an increased self-awareness comes an increased ability to change those assumptions and to be critical of the institutions from which they are derived.

C. Text (and Life) as Performance--The Production of a Scene from a Play

Choose any one of the plays in the Lexington Introduction, or better still a play that is being produced locally.

1. Divide class into groups of three to five and have each group choose a scene which they will enact during the following class. They should be free to adapt the scene by adding contemporary music, making up their own songs, and using costumes and props, but they must follow the action of the play. Their goal is to use whatever dramatic devices they can to persuade the audience of their interpretation, to engage the audience in what might otherwise be a boring scene, to update socially a theme that might seem irrelevant, etc.

2. After each performance (5-10 minutes), the rest of the class will offer a critique, both of the interpretations the group developed and of their techniques of production.

3. Each group should provide a short written justification for the techniques they chose to use, which will include their assumptions about their audiences' literary and general repertoires.

4. In their justifications for their productions, students should address such issues as: What textual/dramatic/comic strategies seem to derive from a historical or cultural repertoire that differs from your own? What parts of the play did you particularly enjoy/understand? Why? What parts were you particularly confused by? How is your interpretation constrained by your general and literary repertoires?

D. The Research Paper: How Can We Discover the Underlying Literary and General Repertoires of Other Readers?

Have students read the appropriate sections in the Introduction to the Essay. You may want to discuss them carefully in class. Then, if appropriate, we suggest you introduce students to the conventions and demands of a formal paper.

1. Introduce class to new MLA format--see the guidelines in the Lexington Introduction. Explain format for first page, footnotes (remember only substantive ones), quotations, and bibliography.

2. Bring various journals and bibliographies to class. Explain such things as continuous pagination, journal binding, journal abbreviations in bibliographies, etc. Divide class into a few groups, each with one bibliography, and have them find a reference on a text of their choice. One member of the group should then write the reference on the blackboard in proper MLA bibliographical format. The rest of the class should check format. (NOTE: This is not an idle task; most students do not know how to use bibliographies and can profit by this instruction.)

3. Consult Reading Texts Chapter 4 for an extended discussion of how students can read critical essays and write a creative, culturally-aware research paper. Also included in Chapter 4 is a sample student research paper with extensive teacher commentary.

4. Take students on a library tour.

a. Contact the reference room or English subject specialist well in advance to arrange a tour for your class.

b. Librarians will be able to give students handouts regarding bibliographies, journals, and books, and if an on-line catalogue is in use, will show students (and teachers if necessary) how to use it.

c. Be sure your tour is a **walking tour**. Students get bored sitting in a room, and need to see the actual location of books in the library. You can also ask students to look up a reference in a bibliography and find it in a journal if they are on a walking tour.

5. Assign the following response statement using the extracts from Williams's Keywords on the polyvalence of words for the beginning of Part IV.

Read Raymond Williams's discussions/definitions of words in which the words clearly do not have just one literal meaning, but in fact seem to have many meanings, a number of which may contradict each other. Come up with two other examples of words that fit this pattern. Feel free to browse through a good dictionary to help you discover such words.

PART IV: THE ROLE OF SIGN SYSTEMS IN CONSTITUTING US AS THINKING SUBJECTS IN OUR CULTURE

A. How Does Language Differ from Itself? Can We Ever Determine "Literal" Meaning?

> Williams, Keywords
> Orwell, "Politics and the English Language"
> Foucault, "The Order of Things"
> Harris, "Women, Baseball, and Words"

Select brief passages from these or other relevant texts that indicate how a word can be defined in a specific way and simultaneously in the opposite or at least in a very different way.

1. Focus on 3–5 words you have given students to read about—at this stage, it is important to confine the analysis to single words or words in a simple sentence, i.e., "My aunt is a butcher." Emphasize that literal meanings are conventional rather than absolute and that they are often difficult or impossible to determine upon close examination of a word.

2. Allow students to ask a lot of questions. They may easily be confused by this exercise and many will want to hold out for "origins" or "real" meanings.

3. Discuss examples of words students have discovered that convey diverse meanings.

4. Explore the implications of recognizing that a word's meanings differ for the analysis of literature, political speeches, television. Gender-related reading is a particular good issue to focus on here.

5. Assign a response statement on Sontag's "Illness as Metaphor" as follows:

A. Analyze the metaphors Sontag uses to describe tuberculosis and cancer. Analyze the relationship of disease metaphors to political philosophy. How can language affect the way people are perceived in a society?

B. Sontag is, of course, offering an interpretation *of disease metaphors in the 19th and 20th centuries. Do you disagree with any of her points?*

B. How Do Metaphors Function in Society?

Have students read sections from the introduction to the essay. Read also the section on Metaphor and Other Figurative Language in the Poetry Introduction.

1. Spend the first half of the class helping students to understand Sontag's points since many students will not fully understand what metaphor is or how it can function on a social level, not just in poetry. Compare and contrast Sontag's analyses of the metaphors of tuberculosis and cancer.

2. Use this class as an opportunity to illustrate that metaphors, like everything else we've been discussing, are culturally situated. Students, for example, will often find it difficult to believe that pallor could have been associated with sexual potency. Comments like this one should be turned back on the class: What is a sign of sexual potency today? Responses will often include having a tan, good muscles, etc. With little prodding, students can see how these signs are equally as arbitrary as pallor.

3. Allow students to discuss personal experiences they have had with family or friends who have had cancer or tuberculosis so that they can, first, analyze how they reacted to the situation and, second, discover if their experiences verify or refute Sontag's analysis.

4. Analyze Sontag's argument rhetorically. Clearly, in her analysis, cancer seems the worse of the two diseases to have, at least from a social perspective. But her argument must be situated historically. She neglects to. mention the social stigma associated with tuberculosis among those of the poorer classes or the slow excruciating death suffered by many TB victims. This, of course, is because she is trying to analyze the diseases as metaphors, but on a number of occasions she does talk much more directly about the reality of having cancer than about the reality of having tuberculosis. Most students will notice this on their own. Probe them as to why they think Sontag's analysis moves in this manner and

whether they think this is a flaw in the book. Perhaps Sontag treats cancer somewhat more seriously because she is removed from the 19th century? Perhaps it is because everyone thinks that the diseases of one's own time are always worse than those of other times. Perhaps Sontag's having cancer herself is a piece of information that may lead some students to take a narrow biographical interpretation of the argument. Sontag's can be seen as one reading, but not the only one, and if students have a tendency to be reductive in their reading strategies, you might want to steer them away from such a question.

5. Assign response statement on contemporary metaphors:

Using Sontag's mode of analysis, discuss three metaphors we use today to describe such things as success, happiness, freedom, sin, etc. Analyze some of the hidden assumptions that underlie these metaphors. What effects might they have on a society that uses them?

C. Discussion of Other Contemporary Metaphors

1. Allow students to find their own examples of contemporary metaphors; some may still be unable to distinguish metaphors from concepts. Let them critique each other's examples with as little guidance from you as possible.

2. Some rather general discussion of sign systems might be appropriate here to help give students a vocabulary for explaining and deconstructing their examples. For example, the eagle is one symbol of the United States, a metaphor for freedom (and one that many of our students write about); it is a signifier with multiple, perhaps contradictory (depending on your political affiliation) signifiers. Though commonly signifying strength, power, independence, sharp-sightedness, it is also a bird of prey, i.e., it kills and eats living things that are smaller than itself. It has also been used on the military standards of many powerful nations, including the Roman Empire, and we all recall that Rome fell. Therefore, the eagle may also signify either military conquests or, perhaps, the eventual downfall of the conqueror.

3. Assign a response statement on analyzing some examples of a contemporary political language.

A. Find a newspaper or magazine article on a current political issue. You should choose two or three major issues so that a number of students will know something about any one of the issues. Discuss the contradictory connotations of at least five metaphors in the article. Students should be asked to read the essays by Barthes and Harris.

B. Since no statement can ever be truly objective, even if it is defined by society as such, you need to try to analyze the assumptions underlying the particular perspective it presents. What do you think the "dominant" ideology is of the article you have chosen to analyze? NOTE: This differs from its main point, i.e., the article may be reporting an American invasion of a small South American country and may be saying that the invasion was a wise and proper action--this is its main point. Its ideology, however, may be much broader based, i.e., that the invasion represented resistance to the spread of Communism by the United States as representative of the progressive free world.

C. Do you feel that the article reflects any "emergent" or repressed ideologies? If so, explain how you are able to discover them.

D. How Do Popular Texts Reflect the Diverse Ideologies of a Culture?

Barthes, "The Photographic Message"
Harris, "Women, Baseball, and Words"
Newspaper and magazine articles on a current political issue

This assignment continues the cultural critique started with Sontag, but also reinforces earlier points about interpretation, developed particularly with Hamlet.

1. By this point, students should be quite adept at finding metaphors, and many are surprised that news articles are filled with them. Allow students to analyze freely and analyze the metaphors they find. You might want to focus on political or gender-specific ones--they seem to be the most accessible. Both Barthes and Harris articulate some of the most significant aspects of current cultural semiotics--that language, images, lifestyles, games, clothing, photographs all carry cultural values. Advertising and newspaper and magazine articles are particularly good for ideological analysis. You may want to spend a very brief time on this segment of the course, preferring to focus more on the literature, but we suggest that it is important to do some work on popular culture. We have provided various suggestions from which you will probably want to make a judicious selection.

2. Analyze whether the articles students selected take overt positions, whether they do it covertly, or whether they try to sound "objective." What kinds of rhetorical strategies are used to claim objectivity? How can they be criticized, i.e., how can students avoid being manipulated by certain kinds of rhetoric?

3. Discuss ways in which the articles present conflicting ideologies. Students are generally quite capable of doing this kind of analysis at this point in the course and will probably need little guidance from the teacher.

159

4. Analyze the implications of becoming more conscious of how language can affect its readers.

5. Assign a response statement on advertising, as follows:

Find two advertisements in magazines or newspapers that use certain metaphors or establish certain signifying systems designed to get you to desire their products. Do they use open persuasion? In what ways are you "taken in" by these tactics; in what ways do you "resist" them? What are the implications of your becoming more conscious of the ways in which advertisements are meant to work on you?

E. How Do Advertisements Reflect Contemporary Ideology?

Again, you may want to spend only a brief time on advertisements, preferring instead to focus on literature. But we do urge that you do some work on contemporary cultural texts of this kind.

1. Establish parallels between the language of advertising and our general language system, including the language of literature. Many students will now begin to notice the arbitrariness of the signifier/signified relationships established in advertising (cheeseburger/sports car; beer/attractive blond woman; water faucets/famous buildings--ancient and modern; perfume/love relationship, etc.). Some will seem less arbitrary than others, however, simply because they have been so conventionalized, the perfume/love association, for example. It is important to make clear that none of these associations is "natural," but that repeated exposure to them can make them seem natural, just as certain meanings of words seem natural to the words themselves. Relate this to previous discussion of "literal" meanings.

2. Explore the ideological assumptions underlying the advertisements such as the notion of a unified self; a continuous, non-arbitrary history; the subservience of women to men; the attractiveness of what is foreign; the superiority of what is American, etc. Analyze how these ideologies often conflict between ads, but also within a single ad. From your analysis, try to distinguish between dominant and emergent ideologies.

3. If there is time, you might try to categorize the types of ads students have found: those that make the viewer the center of the attention; those that define the viewer/individual by the use of the product; those that equate the product with something to which it has no natural relationship etc., (See Judith Williamson, Decoding Advertising, and Reading Texts, Chapter 8.)

PART V: THE IMPLICATIONS OF BECOMING CONSCIOUS OF HOW LANGUAGE, HISTORY, AND CULTURE INFLUENCE OUR READINGS

In this final section, we have in mind the question: What is the best way to climax and conclude an introduction to literature? Just as the opening segment of a course is crucial--Who are all those strange people? What is all this theory?--so too are the final 2-3 weeks. We suggest that you try to reinforce the central theoretical concepts around which the course is organized, and that you end with a bang rather than with a whimper.

Our suggestion is that you have the course culminate in two concentrated segments that focus on reading (necessarily brief) the literature of the nineteenth century and the literature of the last forty years. Our world has been deeply influenced by the currents of thought in the past century--you may have already introduced students to Freud, Barthes, Foucault, three of the most influential minds in the past century; and throughout the Lexington Introduction and this guide, we have stressed the centrality of feminist reading as an especially important variety of strong reading. Feminism, in its various guises has been one of the major forces in our world in the past century. As for contemporary literature, it is one of the scandals of the way English is widely taught that the literature alongside which instructors and students have grown up should be so neglected in introductory courses. So we suggest that a concentration on both Victorian and contemporary writing is a fitting way to bring your course to a climax.

A. In What Ways Can You Gain Knowledge about a Historical Period?

Before starting this segment, you might assign each student a small research assignment: to investigate and report verbally on an aspect of nineteenth-century society that is both relevant to the texts studied and to our own time. Such topics might include: the women's movement, Ibsen's drama, Americans in Europe, political changes in Europe, the decline of the aristocracy, the industrial revolution, religious trends, the New England transcendentalists, agnosticism, Darwinianism, the Pre-Raphaelites, the Catholic Revival, Karl Marx, Irish politics, and so forth. These reports will allow the class to share in both the historical context in which these texts were written and the questions we today may still want to put to those texts.

Texts for this segments of the course might include:

Ibsen, The Wild Duck
Hawthorne, "Young Goodman Brown"
James, "The Real Thing"
Joyce, "The Dead"
Tennyson, "Ulysses/Tithonus"
        "Tears, Idle Tears"
        "Break, Break, Break"
Rossetti, "Song," and "Remember"
Arnold, "To Marguerite"
Hardy, "Ah, Are You Digging on My Grave?"

Arnold, "Dover Beach"
Barrett Browning, "Sonnet 43"
Browning, "My Last Duchess"

1. Three to four reports about the Victorian period should be presented. These are not designed to provide historical information that will give students an objective or correct meaning, but rather to show how texts grow out of particular general and literary ideological conjunctions.

2. Having provided a context for the writing of these texts, next shift to the contemporary reading of nineteenth-century texts. Are the issues these texts raise still with us? How do we respond to them? What questions do we ask of these texts that arise from our ideological conjunction? By this point in the course, your students should be well versed in this dual perspective, and should see meanings as not inherent in these texts as in the interaction between the texts and themselves. We often use John Fowles's novel The French Lieutenant's Woman here--and even if you don't prescribe the novel, as a special (and powerfully relevant) treat, you might show your class the movie and discuss the way it juxtaposes nineteenth-century and contemporary perspectives.

B. Reading Contemporary (Post-Modern) Culture Through Its Literature

In this final segment the goal is to apply the concepts of the course to a selection of texts from the last forty or so years. Texts that are especially good in this section are the contemporary plays, The Gap, Six Characters, and the stories by Munro, Beattie, Barrett, Updike, Atwood, Barth, Barthelme, and Sukenick. It is a paradox that contemporary literature seems much less accessible to contemporary students than literature from the nineteenth or early twentieth centuries. The reasons are complex but explicable and have to do less with the supposed esoteric or difficult nature of the literature or the difficulty of telling what is "good" or "lasting" than with the institutionalization of literary teaching by means of the "canon." If literature matters, then it must matter in the present. It must also be enjoyable. Without pleasure, no texts are going to come alive in their readers' minds or lives.

Consequently, we suggest that this final segment be an exercise in informed jouissance, to use Barthes's term. The pleasure of reading should be stressed-- the predominantly comic character of the texts we suggest will help--and students should as well be encouraged to relate their pleasure (and puzzlement) to wider cultural experiences--to feelings of mobility, decenteredness, dislocation, unpredictability, or to their own sense of what it is like to grow up (Barthes), not quite know what your real self is (Pirandello), be overwhelmed by the crazy details of life (Sukenick). Then, too, the more reassuring stories--by Beattie or Munro for instance--may cater to and lead to a discussion on the power of nostalgia and the craving for an order that we sometimes locate back in our own, or our society's, past.

Finally--to repeat some (by now) truisms--the aim of this segment, like the aim of the course as a whole, is not to get agreement, or firm answers. It is to raise questions, to get students to see where those questions come from, how they are embodied and focused in the reading experience, and how their introduction to literature is always (or, some of us are wont to say, always already) an introduction to experiences that go beyond literature. Reading texts well means learning to read the world and ourselves well.

1 2 3 4 5 6 7 8 9 0